J. Smith

Twelve Sermons, upon the Following Subjects ..

J. Smith

Twelve Sermons, upon the Following Subjects ..

ISBN/EAN: 9783337243753

Printed in Europe, USA, Canada, Australia, Japan

Cover: Foto ©Lupo / pixelio.de

More available books at **www.hansebooks.com**

TWELVE SERMONS,

UPON

The following SUBJECTS:

I. The Divinity of *Christ*.
II. *Jepthah*'s Vow.
III. The good *Samaritan*.
IV. A proper and an improper Conformity to the World.
V. Prayer—what it is, and what it is not.
VI. *Solomon*'s Request.
VII. *Agur*'s Request.
VIII. Plain Truth.
IX. Truth dissembled.
X. The natural Desire of long Life.
XI. The Folly and Danger of despising Religion.
XII. The Penitent upon the Cross.

By the Rev. J. SMITH, M. A.

Chaplain in Ordinary to his MAJESTY.

———————

LONDON:

PRINTED by M. HARRISON, No. 2, RED LYON COURT, FLEET STREET.
MDCCLXXVI.

PREFACE.

I WAS advised by many kind Friends to delay the Publication of these Discourses a few Months longer; but the Opinion of some of my Subscribers corresponding with my own Ideas of Delicacy in in a Matter of this Kind — I hope that I have not done wrong in publishing them now.

I considered it as a Duty — to be so far *particular* in the Acknowledgment of *Obligations* upon *this Occasion*, as to print the Names of my Subscribers,

PREFACE.

Subscribers, whose Candour *after* Publication, will, I doubt not, prove *equal* to their Civility and Generosity *before*.

The first, eighth, and ninth Sermons, are partly taken from two eminent *French* Divines. They have, however, been preached before very distinguished Congregations, and it was particularly recommended to me to give them a Place in this printed Collection.

I may say of the Sermon upon the Divinity of *Christ* (what a late Writer says of his own religious Treatise) that it is "an Abstract only "— designed to raise a proper Attention, and to create a Desire, in " young

PREFACE.

"young or doubting Persons, to pursue the Subject—till the Mind finds Reason to be satisfied in *that* Certainty of Evidence the *whole* produces," on which this essential Article of the christian Faith is founded.

The Rest of the Discourses (except in Matters strictly doctrinal) are taken from Life rather than from *Books*—from *Observation* rather than from *Reading*. I have *endeavoured* to represent the World as it *now* is—to make all possible *Allowance* for Error and Indiscretion—to give every possible *Commendation* to Principles and Conduct, lovely and of good Report. In a Word; whatever

PREFACE.

ever Imperfections may be discovered in the following slender Performance, when examined with a critical Attention — I hope it will appear — that I (at least) *wish* Religion *well* — that I *wish* my Fellow-Mortals *well* — *wish* them to be happy *Here* — but at all Events to take Care that they become so *Hereafter*, through their *own best* Endeavours, *perfected* by the Merits and Mediation of *Jesus Christ*.

LONDON, MAY 6, 1776.

CONTENTS.

CONTENTS.

SERMON I.
Upon the DIVINITY of CHRIST.

John i. 1, 2. *In the Beginning was the Word, and the Word was with God, and the Word was God. The same was in the Beginning with God.* Page 3.

SERMON II.
Upon JEPTHAH'S VOW.

Judges xi. 30. *And Jepthah vowed a Vow unto the Lord.* p. 19.

SERMON III.
Upon the GOOD SAMARITAN.

Luke x. 36, 37. *Which now of these three thinkest thou was Neighbour unto him who fell amongst the Thieves? And he said, he that shewed Mercy on him: Then said Jesus unto him, go—and do thou likewise.* P. 37.

SERMON

CONTENTS.

SERMON IV.
Upon a PROPER and an IMPROPER CONFORMITY to the WORLD.

Prov. xxix. 25. *The Fear of Man bringeth a Snare.* p. 51.

SERMON V.
Upon PRAYER—what it is, and what it is not.

Pfalm v. 3. *I will direct my Prayer unto Thee.* p. 65.

SERMON VI.
Upon SOLOMON's REQUEST.

1. Kings iii. 10. *And the Speech pleafed the Lord that* Solomon *had afked this Thing.* p. 81.

SERMON VII.
Upon AGUR's REQUEST.

Prov. xxx. 7, 8, 9. *Two Things have I required of Thee, deny me them not before I die:*

CONTENTS.

I die: Remove far from me Vanity and Lies; give me neither Poverty nor Riches; feed me with Food convenient for me: Lest I be full and deny Thee, and say who is the Lord? or lest I be poor and steal, and take the Name of my God in vain. p. 97.

SERMON VIII.

Upon PLAIN TRUTH.

Matt. ii. 2. *Where is he that is born King of the* Jews? p. 511.

SERMON IX.

TRUTH dissembled.

Matt. ii. 5. *And they said unto him—in* Bethlehem *of* Judea. p. 129.

SERMON X.

Upon the NATURAL DESIRE of LONG LIFE.

Job xlii. 16. *After this lived* Job *an hundred and forty Years, and saw his Sons*

CONTENTS.

Sons and his Sons Sons, even four Generations. p. 145.

SERMON XI.

Upon the FOLLY and DANGER of despising RELIGION.

1 Thess. iv. 8. *He therefore that despiseth—despiseth not Man—but God.* p. 165.

SERMON XII.

Upon the PENITENT upon the CROSS.

Luke xxiii. 42, 43. *And he said unto Jesus—Lord, remember me when thou comest into thy Kingdom: And Jesus said unto him, Verily I say unto thee—to Day shalt thou be with me—in Paradise.*
p. 181.

A LIST

OF THE

SUBSCRIBERS NAMES.

A.

Francis Annesley, Esq.
James Anderson, Esq.
Mr. Acton.
Mr. Agutter.
Mr. Andrews.
Mrs. Armetage.
Mr. William Arnold
Mr. Atkins.

B.

Right Rev. Lord Bishop of Bristol.
Sir William Boyer, Bart.
Rev. William Backhouse, D. D. Archdeacon of Canterbury.
Rev. Lewis Boisdaune, Chaplain in Ordinary to his Majesty.
Rev. Dr. Baker.
John Batley, Esq.
Jeremiah Batley, Esq.
Mrs. Batley.
Thomas Beach, Esq.
James Brown, Esq. Fellow Commoner of Catharine Hall, Cambridge.
John Browning, Esq.
Christopher Buckle, Esq.
Rev. Mr. Bethune, M. A.
Rev. Mr. Bodicoate, M. A. Vicar of Westerham, in Kent.
Mrs. Martha Bates.
Mrs. Bayford.
Mr. Bellet.
Mr. James Bentham, of Catharine Hall, Cambridge.
Mr. Thomas Berwick.
Mrs. Biddle.
Mrs. Bolton.
Mr. Bridges.
Mr. John Brockbank.
Mr. Brown.
Mr. Isaac Brown.
Mr. John Buckle.
Mr. Edward Butler.
Mr. Edward Butler. jun.
Mr. Buy.
Mr. G. Buy.

C.

Hon. and most Rev. his Grace the Lord Archbishop of Canterbury.
Right

SUBSCRIBERS NAMES.

Right Hon. Lady Mary Carr.
Right Hon. Lord Cockrane.
Hon. John Cockrane.
Hon. James Cockrane.
Rev. J. Chevallier, B. D. Master of St. John's College, Cambridge.
Rev. Augustus Calvert, L. L. D. Fellow of the Society of Antiquaries.
Richard Clay, Esq.
John Cheinock, Esq. of Trinity College, Oxford.
Robert Cooke, Esq. Fellow Commoner of Catharine Hall, Cambridge.
John Carellius, Esq.
Mrs. Carellius.
William Caslon, Esq.
Mrs. Caslon.
Rev. Charles Coates, M. B.
Rev. Charles Coxwell, M. A. Rector of Barnesley, in Gloucestershire.
Mr. James Coxwell.
Mr. Charles Carpenter.
Mr. William Caslon.
Mr. Henry Caslon.
Mr. John Chandler.
Mr. Chevors.
Mr. Clifsold.
Mr. John Cooper.
Mr. Thomas Cooper.

D.

Rev. Samuel Dennis, D.D. President of St. John's College, Oxford.
Rev. William Dalton, President of Catharine Hall, Cambridge.
George Devon, Esq.
Rev. Tho. Dalton, M. A. Fellow of Queen's College, Oxford.
Francis Dawson, M. A. Fellow of Catharine Hall, Cambridge.
Rev. Mr. Disturnell, M. A.
Rev. Samuel Dobson, M. A. Fellow of Catharine Hall, Cambridge.
Mr. R. Davenport, of St. John's College, Oxford.
Mr. Darwell.
Mr. Dawson,
Mr. Dibbs.

E.

James Esdaile, jun. Esq.
Mrs. Esdaile.
William Eamonson, M. A. Fellow of Catharine Hall, Cambridge.
Mr. Ellis.

F.

Rev. Dr. Francklin, Chaplain in Ordinary to his Majesty.

Rev.

SUBSCRIBERS NAMES.

Rev. Dr. Finch, Fellow of St. John's College, Oxford.
Rev. Francis Finch, B. D.
Mr. Richard Farmer.
Mr. James Farrer.
Mrs. Feild.
Mr. Field.
Mrs. Field.
Mrs Mary Field.
Mr. Fielder.
Mr. Freeman.
Mr. Fulton.

G.
Rev. Dr. Glass, Chaplain in Ordinary to his Majesty.
Robert Gosling, Esq.
Edward Green, Esq.
Abraham Guyott, Esq.
Rev. Philip Gardnar, B. D. Fellow of Catharine Hall, Cambridge.
Rev. Mr. Goldwyer, Vicar of Letcomb Regis, in Berkshire.
Rev. Mr. Graves, Rector of Hatfield, in Hertfordshire.
Mr. John Gidley.
Mr. Given.
Mr. Griffiths.
Mrs. Guichenet.

H.
Right Hon. the Earl of Hertford, Lord Chamberlain of his Majesty's Houshold.
George Hayter, Esq.
Rev. Mr. Hand, M. A. Vicar of St. Giles's, Cripplegate.
Rev. Peter Hawker, M. A. Rector of Woodchester, in Gloucestershire.
Rev. Mr. Hayter.
Rev. G. G. Hayter.
Rev. Mr. Heckstall, M. A. Rector of St. Ann's, Aldersgate.
Rev. Mr. Hinckley.
Rev. Mr. Humphries.
Mr. G. Halifax.
Mr. Harper.
Mr Harris.
Mr. Hartley.
Mr. Hartwell.
Mr. John Hawker.
Miss Hawker.
Mr. William Hopkins.

J.
Edward Jones, Esq.
Rev. Thomas Johnson, B. A. Fellow of Catharine Hall, Cambridge.
Benjamin Ingham, B. A. Fellow of Catharine Hall, Cambridge.
Rev. Humphry Jefferies.

K.
Rev. Dr. Kettilby, Vicar of St. Bartholemew the Less.
J. Kirkman

SUBSCRIBERS NAMES.

J. Kirkman, Esq.
Mr. Francis Knight.
Mr. Kearsley.
Mr. William Knapp.
Mrs. Kewell

L.

Right Rev. Lord Bishop of London.
James Lowther, Esq.
Samuel Lewis, Esq.
Henry Lumley, Esq.
Rev. Marmaduke Lawson, M A. Fellow of Catharine Hall, Cambridge.
Mrs. Le Breton.
Mr. Leigh.
Mr. William Lewis.

M.

Rev. Thomas Marriot, D. D. Chaplain in Ordinary to his Majesty.
Rev. Robert Markham, D. D. Rector of St. Mary, Whitechapel.
Gilbert Mellefont, Esq. of Christ-church, Oxford.
Thomas Moore, Esq.
Rev. Jonathan Morgan, M. A. Rector of Hedley in Surry.
Rev. Mr. Myers.
Mrs. Murray.
Mr. Mayhew.
Mr. Meadows.
Mr. Francis Moore.
Miss E. Morris.

Mr. Morrell, of St. John's Colledge, Oxford.

N.

Mrs. Newton.
John Nash, Esq.
William Naylor, Esq.
Mr. Thomas Tregonwell Napier.
Mr. Newman.

P.

Right Rev. Lord Bishop of Peterborough.
Nathaniel Peach, Esq.
Samuel Peach, Esq.
Benjamin Peach, Esq.
Edward Peach, Esq.
William Gaisford Peach, Esq.
William Pocock, Esq.
Mrs. Pocock.
Rev. Henry Peach, B. D. Fellow of St. John's College, Oxford.
William Peirson, Esq. Fellow Commoner of Catharine Hall, Cambridge.
Rev. Charles Plucknett, B. D. Fellow of St. John's College, Oxford.
Rev. John Peddle of St. Mary Hall, Oxford.
Rev. William Pickering, M. A. Fellow of Sidney Sussex College Cambridge.

Rev.

SUBSCRIBERS NAMES.

Rev. Mr. Piggott, Fellow of St. John's College, Oxford.
Rev. Mr. Pitts.
Rev. Charles Prescot, M.A. Fellow of Catharine Hall, Cambridge.
Mr. Page.
Miss Pierce.
Mr. Pope.
Mr. Prickett.

R.

Edward Reynolds, Esq.
Mr. William Ringsted.
Mr. Ruddle.

S.

Lady Anderson Shirley.
—— Skeet, L.L.D.
George Schoen, Esq. of St. John's College, Oxford.
Thomas Shurmur, Esq.
Edward Skettell, Esq. of Christ Church, Oxford.
Robert Skettell, Esq. of Christ Church, Oxford.
Rev. John Spicer, M.A. of Reading.
Rev. Mr. Sturgis, M.A. Vicar of St. Mary's in Reading.
Rev. Mr. Sisson.
Hugh Smith, M.D.
Mrs. Smith.
Mr. Salkeld.
Mrs. Salkeld.
Mr. Sanagen.

Mr. Sandland.
Mrs. Savage.
Mrs. Scrimshire.
Mr. Sealy.
Mr. Secker.
Mr. Sherwood, junior.
Mrs. Shepley.
Mr. Thomas Shurmur.
Mr. James Sibbald.
Mrs. Smart.
Mr. Robert Smith.
Miss Mary Smith.
Miss E. Smith.
Mr. Smithson.
Mr. Snowdon.
Mrs. Spencer.
Mr. Spotswood.
Mr. William Stevens.
Mr. John Stevens.
Mrs. Henry Stevens.
Mr. Strong.
Mr. Swinscoe.

T.

Right Hon. Earl Talbot, Lord Steward of his Majesty's Household.
Miss Talbot.
Hon. Miss Mary Tryon, Maid of Honour to her Majesty.
William Temple, Esq.
Lewis Tregonwell, Esq. of Trinity College, Oxford.
George Trenchard, Esq. of Merton College, Oxford.

U.

SUBSCRIBERS NAMES.

U.

Rev. Benjamin Underwood, M. A.. Rector of East Barnet.
Mrs. Vancourt.

W.

William Whitehead, Esq. Poet Laureat.
Rev. Thomas Wright, Chaplain in Ordinary to his Majesty.
Rev. Mr. Winstanley, M. A. Prebendary of St. Paul's.
John Wade, Esq.
―― Walford, Esq.
Thomas Wigsell, Esq.
Mrs. Wigsell.
Atwood Wigsell, Esq.
St. John Wessell Wigsell, Esq.
―― Willis, Esq.
Rev. Mr. Whalley, M. A. Rector of St. Margaret Pattens.
Rev. Mr. Wray, M. A. Rector of Darley in Derbyshire.
Rev. John Wilsford, M.A. Fellow of Catharine Hall, Cambridge.
Rev. Joshua Waterhouse, B. A. Fellow of Catharine Hall, Cambridge.
Rev. Joshua Wood, B. A. Fellow of Catharine Hall, Cambridge.
Mr. Thomas Wigsell of St. John's College, Oxford.
Miss Wigsell.
Rev. Mr. Wendeborn.
Mr. Samuel Wathen, Jun.
Mr. Webb.
Mr. Williams.

Y.

Rev. Lowther Yates, B. D. Fellow of Catharine Hall, Cambridge.

ERRATA.

Page 90, line 11, for *Serenity* read *Sincerity*.
108, ― 19, for *Vine* read *Pine*.
152, ― 15, for *desirest* read *desiredst*.
174, ― 6, for *Purity* read *Parity*.

SERMON I.

UPON THE

DIVINITY OF CHRIST.

B

SERMON

UPON

PRIVATE PRAYER

SERMON I.

JOHN i. 1, 2.

In the Beginning was the Word, and the Word was with God, and the Word was God.

The same was in the Beginning with God.

I Shall, with, I hope, a becoming Reverence to so sacred a Subject, presume, in the ensuing Sermon, to speak of the Divinity of Jesus Christ; wishing hereby to prove from the plain Authorities of Scripture, and from clear unprejudiced Reasoning—that our Lord was, from the Glory, and the very Spirit and Essence of his Ministry upon Earth, manifestly God.

The first shining Part of our Lord's Ministry is — that he was foretold and promised to Men almost ever since the World existed. Scarcely had *Adam* fallen, but is shewed him (tho' at a great Distance) this kind Recoverer. In succeeding Ages God appeared, as it were, to be unmindful of any Thing else, but to prepare Men for the Arrival of this Saviour. In short our Lord was foretold by all People — declared for Four Thousand Years by a long Chain of Prophets — figured out by all the Ceremonies of the Law — and wished for by the Just of all Ages. Neither was all this for the Sake of some particular Event only: He was to be the Resource of a condemned World — A Law-giver of divers People — the Light of Nations — the Salvation of *Israel*. But what a Snare for the Religion of all Times — if Preparations so great and important specified a Creature merely human — of thofe Times efpecially, when the Credulity of the World fo eafily fuffered Men of uncommon Notions or uncommon Abilities — to rank as Gods.

John the Baptift — in Order to prevent Idolatry in his Nation — is ever heard to fay — I am not he whom you expect. Our Lord, on the Contrary, whom Four Thoufand Years of Figures and Prophecies had acknowledged — at Length comes in great Virtue and Power. He performs Miracles which no other Perfon ever did before him, and inftead of preventing the People from worfhipping him — he declares himfelf to be equal with God, and fuffers the World to render divine Honours to him. If this was an idolatrous Worfhip, Mankind feem to be by no Means refponfible for it.

In the Ages before the Coming of our Lord — there appeared many very extraordinary Men, whom the Almighty feemed to have made, as it were, Confidants of his

Virtue and his Power: And yet when we attend to this Matter closely, we find that all these extraordinary Men carried about them Marks of Dependence and Weakness: Our Lord, on the Contrary, performs the most surprising Miracles with a Facility all puissant — and with a Sovereignty wholly independent.

Again, how glorious are the Circumstances before unheard of in any one — which compose the Course of our Lord's mortal Life! Conceived by the Operation of the Holy Ghost, he is born of a pure Virgin. Scarcely is he born, but celestial Legions fill the Air with Songs of Triumph, and assure us that this Birth renders to God his Glory, and Peace to Men. A little afterwards, a new Star conducts to his Cradle wise Men from the East: A just and an holy Woman announces his future Glory: The Doctors being assembled together behold, with Astonishment, his Infancy more wise and understanding

standing than the Wisdom and Experience of old Age.

In Proportion as he advances in Years, his Glory discovers itself the more. *John Baptist* humbles himself before him—Heaven opens itself upon his Head—the affrighted Devils cannot abide his Presence—the Father of Heaven declares that he is his well-beloved Son, and proposes him as the living and eternal Law, in commanding Mankind to listen to him.

If from *Tabor* we pass over to *Mount Calvary*—the Place where all the Reproaches and Cruelties exercised upon our Lord exhausted themselves; all Nature in confusion acknowledges him even here as it's Author, and confesses his Divinity. He arises from his Grave three Days after, not by Means of any foreign Help, or that he might die again; but by his own Power, and that he might be in Possession henceforth of a Life immortal. To finally close the Scene,

Scene, our Lord afcendeth into Heaven. It is not a Chariot of Fire that conveys him thither, in the Twinkling of an Eye — he raifes himfelf with Majefty — the Angels come to meet him, and promife him a fecond Appearance upon Earth, when he fhall be encompaffed with Glory and Immortality.

In Footfteps like thefe who fhould not gladly trace out the God of Heaven? In him, who after having converfed with Men, in order to recover them from their Wanderings and their Mifery, left them and their World, and renewed the Poffeffion of his heavenly Glory. Surely, the exceedingly great Luftre of our Lord's Miniftry would unavoidably be to us an Occafion of Idolatry, if he was not more than mere Man. As alfo would the very Spirit and Effence of his Miniftry be an unavoidable Snare to our Innocence.

No one has ever yet denied that Jefus Chrift was an holy Man. What Man indeed ever

SERMON I.

ever appeared upon Earth, in whom all People remarked so strong Characters of Innocence and Sanctity? I might say, so great Indifference for the World, so great Love for Virtue, so great Zeal for the Glory of God, so great Ardour for the Salvation of Mankind? We may add to all this, the total Exemption of those Weaknesses, which we know to be inseparable from mere human Nature. Now if Jesus Christ be thus holy, he must be God — He must needs be such, as to the Doctrine which he bequeathed to us, whether we consider it as regarding his almighty Father or ourselves.

If Christ is nothing but a simple Embassador from God — he is not come but to shew to Nations an *idolatrous Unity* of the *divine Essence*. In the next Place, our Lord must have made use of evil Means for the Discharge of his Ministry. *Moses* and the Prophets, charged with a similar Mission, never ceased to publish that the Lord Almighty is

one,

one, without ever making a Comparison between themselves and the supreme Being: Whereas Christ seldom ceases to equal himself with his Father. — He says that he is descended from Heaven, and taken from the Bosom of God — that he existed before all Things — that the Father and himself are one. In every Thing indeed he compares himself with the great Sovereign of all Worlds. The *Jews* murmur and reproach him for these Expressions. So far from denying them, he confirms them all in the Midst of Reproaches, and does this too in a Language affronting and impious, if his Equality and Comparison with his Father do not inform and justify him. Our Lord surely is not come upon the Earth (if he is merely Man) but to offend the *Jews principally*, in giving them an Opportunity at least of believing that he compares himself with the most High: He is not come but to seduce the *Nations*, in causing them to worship him

after

after his Death — He is not come but to disperse a fresh Darkness throughout the Universe. All those great Advantages which the World has been promised to derive from the Ministry of Jesus Christ do, in this Case, center themselves in seeing Mankind plunged into a new Kind of Idolatry, and all the future Magnificence of the Gospel so strongly foretold by the Prophets — must finally be seen to have only tended to form and encourage that dangerous Sect of *Socinians*. But seeing the Manner in which he speaks of his Father, the Equality which he assumes upon most Occasions with his Father — this necessarily establishes the Glory of his eternal Original.

Suppose we next consider our Lord's Doctrine, with Regard to Men. This too must needs establish at least the *Verity* of his *divine* Birth. What Wisdom, what Sanctity, what plain Sublimity in such his Doctrine! Every Thing there is worthy of Reason, and of of the moſt profound Philoſophy: Every Thing there is proportioned to the Miſery, and at the ſame Time to the Excellency, of Man. Remark thoſe Duties of Love and mutual Dependence which he requires of Men one towards another. He enjoins us alſo to love him — to ſeek in him our Happineſs — to refer to him ourſelves and our Actions in like Manner as he teaches us to refer to his Father. But if he be not God, his Doctrine ſo divine, ſo admired even by Heathens — is nothing more than an horrid Mixture of Impiety, of Pride, and Folly; ſeeing he himſelf, being nothing but a mere Man, is deſirous of uſurping the Place of God in our Hearts. Nay more — whilſt the true God appeared to be contented with the Sacrifices of Bulls and of Goats — Chriſt for himſelf is deſirous that we ſacrifice even our own Lives; that we give up ourſelves to Death and Martyrdom for the Glory of his Name. But if he be not the Author of our Lives,

Lives, what Right can he have to require them at our Hands? His Religion is then a Religion of Blood and Barbarity only — the generous Martyrs of his Religion have then proved themselves only Cowards and Fanatics; and the Defenders of Justice and of the Glory of Christ's Divinity, only Tyrants and Persecutors. Can the Ear of Man listen to these Blasphemies without Horror?

I cannot close this important Subject without begging your Attention a little longer, whilst we consider the Spirit of our Lord's Ministry in those Graces and Blessings which the Universe has received from him. He declares that he is come to deliver all Men from eternal Death. He makes us from Enemies become the Children of God — He opens Heaven to us, and assures us, (upon easy Conditions) of a final, certain Possession thereof: He nourishes us from his own Body — he washes us from our Sins, in applying to us the Price of his own Blood:

Blood: In a Word, he calls himself our Way, our Truth, our Life, our Redemption. But as a mere Man, can he possibly be the Source of so great Graces and Benefits to other Men? Or is it not to be feared that as a Man becoming so useful and necessary to Mankind, he is become, at Length, their Idol?

See then to what impious and dangerous Lengths Infidelity is capable of carrying us. I hope that this is a Character applicable to none amongst us. And indeed mere Points of Faith should, perhaps, constitute but a small Part of Preaching; as every Preacher in a christian Land may, with Reason, in general conclude — that he has no Hearers, but what are Believers. Sometimes, however, it may be both useful and seasonable to treat of the Doctrines of Faith, especially when, as in the present Discourse, we can mix them with the equally important Doctrines of Love and Obedience. I will only beg

SERMON I.

beg Leave to add this Argument in Opposition to Incredulity.—that if it is an Error to believe that Jesus Christ is God,—it is an Error which was born with the Christian Church—it is an Error which has raised the whole Edifice—it is an Error which has formed so many Martyrs—it is an Error which has, in a Manner, converted the whole Universe. And ever let us conclude, that Piety and Reverence towards this our Saviour both God and Man—is the deep Spirit of our Religion—that nothing is solid or permanent but what we build upon this Foundation: And the principal Homage which our Lord requires of us is—that his Way be the Model of our own, so that at Length being conformed to a Resemblance of him here, we may finally be of the Number of those who shall be Partakers of his eternal Glory, To whom with the Father and the holy Spirit—three Persons but one

one God—be ascribed all Honour and Power, Might, Majesty, and Dominion— now and for evermore. Amen.

SERMON II.

UPON

JEPTHAH's VOW.

PREACHED

Before the UNIVERSITY of CAMBRIDGE, on SUNDAY, MARCH, 20, 1774.

C

SERMON II.

JUDGES xi. 30. first Part.

And Jepthah *vowed a Vow unto the Lord.*

THE Words of his Vow were these. " If thou shalt without Fail—deliver the Children of *Ammon* into mine Hands; then it shall be, that whatsoever cometh forth of the Doors of my House to meet me when I return in Peace from the Children of *Ammon* shall surely be the Lord's, and I will offer it up for a Burnt-Offering." On his Return, after the completest Victory to his own House at *Mizpeh*—behold, his Daughter came out to meet him,

him, and she was his only Child. This is a Scene which must needs awaken our tender — humane Feelings, and prepare us for the Exercise of all imaginable Compassion towards the afflicted Parties.

Picture to yourselves a Man returning on the Wings of Victory — having totally subdued an Enemy who had created so great Fear in those who had sent for this Deliverer from a Country — whither they had most unjustly banished him. Fancy to yourselves a Man thus returning not only with Victory in his Hands, but also with Gratitude in his Soul to that Almighty Arm which had wrought Success. Suppose him too within Sight of his own House, where he expected to receive the Congratulations of his nearest Friends — to impart to them likewise in Return, some of his overflowing Joy: In particular you are to suppose that he had an amiable and a dutiful Daughter to meet on this Occasion, the only Child of his

his fond, parental Bosom. Such was *Jepthah*'s Situation! And had it not been for that rash and inconsiderate Vow which he made before his Conquest, we might have followed him into his House, and have fancied every Thing that was joyful and happy. But through Means of this fatal Resolution, we must make a Transition from a supposed Picture of perfect human Happiness, to one of (in Reality) perfect human Wretchedness. This very *Jepthah*, tho' Conquerer in the Field, is now on a sudden made a Coward; nay a Captive of, and by himself too. Lo! his Daughter came out first to meet him with Timbrels and with Dances. Here began his contrast—Wretchedness. At the Sight of her he rent his Cloaths, and wrapped up in Victory and Joy as he before was, he breaks out into a truly mournful Alas—*Alas, my Daughter, thou hast brought me very low,* and instead of viewing you as my first

Sharer of my Triumphs, *thou art even* one *of them who trouble me; for I have opened my Mouth unto the Lord, and I cannot go back.* What such a Man must feel on an Occasion like this, would, I believe, be difficult to express. The very Rehearsal of the Matter to us who were not concerned in the History — is enough to melt Nature into all that can be suggested by a generous Pity, or a sympathizing Heart. Those may, probably, feel most, who bear the venerable Name of Parent, and the Story is not made the less affecting, by the surprizing Resignation of the fair Victim. Her Duty to her Father — her Readiness to be given up — was a singular Proof surely of her Goodness — but this is a Circumstance which must needs affect our Tenderness more, than if she had broken out into Invectives against a rash Father, and had become an unwilling Sacrifice: Instead of which she never once blames *Jepthah* for

the

the Vow that he had made, but on the Contrary — urges the Fulfillment of it — so long as her Father was returned safe and succesful, she was ready to suffer *according to what had proceeded out of his Mouth.*

This History being thus far laid open — I shall now venture to proceed to that Part of it which most of all belongs to us — the Consideration of the Vow itself: How far *Jepthah* may be blamed or excused both in the making or in the fulfilling of it, which will naturally instruct us with Regard to Vows and Resolutions of our own.

In the Days of *Jepthah* Vows were considered as lawful and binding, and few Things of Consequence were undertaken without some sacred Resolve. And when we read of the Slaughters and Troubles and Superstitions of those Days, and how deliberately Thousands were taken and slain — we must cease to judge of the Instance before us altogether as Christians. Yet make what Allowances we will — *Jepthah* certainly went beyond the Customs and Errors even of his own mistaken Times. Sacrifices we know were wont to be made unto the Lord, and with very pious Intentions — but then it was the Incense of Rams or of Bullocks and of He-Goats, else of the tender and innocent Lamb. *Isaac*, it is true, was destined to be offered up, and by a Command from Heaven too — and Faith's prevailing in this Instance was justly imputed unto *Abraham* as Righteousness; yet the Trial seems to be thought too hard an one by the Lord for a *Man* to offer up his *only Son*: For when Faith had so far subdued the Powers of natural Affection as to bring *Abraham* with his Son to the Place where he was appointed to be slain — an Angel's Voice was heard from Heaven to cry out to *Abraham*, whose Hand was now stretched forth, and in Possession of the Knife prepared for the Slaughter — *lay not thine Hand upon the Lad*. Nay, a Sacrifice of this Sort was

not

not only supposed by the Lord to be most afflicting to a Parent, and indeed Injustice towards the Child — but we may collect I think — that as it was not permitted to be made in the Case of *Isaac* — so in future Times it should have been considered (independently of Nature) as an Act highly offensive in the Sight of God. As a *Jew* was prevented, and by Heaven too prevented — from committing it — a *Jew* should certainly have been taught, even *Jepthah*, to have kept back his rash and inconsiderate Vow with Respect to a fellow Creature, and to have confined it to the Sacrifice of a Ram. And yet methinks our Candor is strongly addressed on the Side of *Jepthah*. His Call to engage against the Children of *Ammon* was a very singular one. He was in Banishment, and invited to return even to fight for, and to rule over, those who banished him. Feel for a Man thus situated: And when he had actually received *the Spi-*

rit

rit *of the Lord* as his Encourager and Supporter, fancy his religious Gratitude so much excited, as to make him think himself acting with a Duty equal to the Greatness of the Occasion, in offering up, in Case of Victory, one of his own Species, nay, one of his own Family — that he might have considered a common Sacrifice too small a Token of so extraordinary an Honour — Gratitude too limited for so great a Share of Mercy. This I say not in Justification of the Vow itself — for it cannot, it must not be countenanced — I mean it only as some Excuse for the unhappy Man who made it. Indeed *Jepthah* seems to be situated in this Matter much like St. *Paul* touching a mistaken Conscience. His Persecutions no Christian must attempt to justify, tho' many Arguments may be urged in Favour of the misled Persecutor. So with Regard to *Jepthah*, when we reflect upon what is recorded of his Disposition and Behaviour

haviour and Principles in general — we cannot avoid in a great Meaſure excuſing him as to the intentional Part of his Vow. Had it been made through Cruelty and Wantonneſs — had he meant to ſport with the Life of a fellow Creature — he would doubtleſs have ſought for ſuch a Victim from Home — not at his own Houſe, which contained Servants who had, probably, by their Fidelity, gained his Eſteem — and beſides theſe a Daughter, an only Child, who being a Perſon ſo nearly concerned in her Father's Joys and Succeſſes was likelieſt too to come out firſt to meet him. And thus it even happened: A Circumſtance, which at the ſame Time that it convinces us of God's peculiar Diſapprobation of the Oath itſelf — increaſes likewiſe our Pity towards the afflicted Father — who ſuffered, I ſuppoſe, all that Man could ſuffer on this Side the Grave. How muſt all his Glory which he had juſt acquired

quired in the Field — be at once converted into Shame of the moſt tormenting Kind; and the Laurels of Victory — into a Crown of Thorns!

But leaving *Jepthah* as far as regards his making this Vow, let us briefly touch upon the Impropriety of his fulfilling it.

That Men ſhould pay a ſacred Attention to Vows or Oaths, in which Religion or the Happineſs of the World is concerned — is a Doctrine which every good and honeſt Man muſt needs inculcate: Nay, whatever we engage our Faith and Promiſe to, whether private Perſons or Society be concerned — provided that ſuch Engagement be founded on moral Virtue or moral Honeſty; they are the worſt of Men, who ſhrink back when it is in their Power to fulfil it. But when Men make Vows in themſelves ridiculous — injurious to Society, and contrary to the Laws of Religion and Morality — let ſuch Men, at the Time that they are about to execute

execute their Vow from a false Scruple of Conscience, or from a false Notion of Honour—rather afflict themselves that they had ever made such Vow at all, and forbear from fulfilling it—than after they have fulfilled it, to carry about them the perpetual Sense of Injury done to those who have suffered by it.

What are our Thoughts of the Tetrarch *Herod*—who for passing a few Hours in lawful Dissipation with *Herodias*'s Daughter—was led to offer her so far as the Half of his Kingdom. Doubtless, he expected that her Request would have been a lucrative one, and when she asked the Baptist's Head in a Charger—he was sorry; yet so idle were his Notions of Honour (for Conscience could no Ways be here concerned) that he suffered his Humanity to fall so great a Sacrifice to it, as even to order that *John* should be beheaded. Now if *Herod* had done wisely, should he not have reproved *Herodias*'s Daughter, at least with saying, *" thou*

" knowest

"*knowest not what thou askest,*" and have left himself to have reflected upon the Folly of Promises or Vows, which make Room for the Exercise of Cruelty and Wrong—without putting his own into Execution at the Expence of the Life of so good and valuable a Man as *John* the Baptist.

And let us instance next, on the Side of a scrupulous Conscience—in the Case of *Jepthah*, who would surely have been a wiser, a happier, and a better Man, if he had permitted his Conscience to have dispensed with the *executive* Part of his Vow, and to have exercised it's *Stings* respecting the *making* of it *only*.

Vows and Resolutions like *Jepthah*'s are indeed unknown to our Times of Revelation, and true Worship which admits of no Sacrifice but that of a broken and a contrite Heart: Yet it is a very displeasing and a very faulty Custom amongst us to load our Consciences with idle Vows and rash Resolutions

tions—so as to lay the greatest Foundation of Unhappiness. In Things that are lovely and of good Report we oftentimes teach our Consciences to evade; but in Things trifling, wrong, or mischievous to the common Good:—we easily become Slaves to this misguided Conscience, 'till at last, when we have shewed ourselves (as we think) Men of firm Principles and Resolution by executing some mad Resolve—we make *ourselves* wretched, as well as *those*, to whom we have proved so cruelly and foolishly resolute. Vows and Resolutions are always made in some *Excess of Passion*; but seldom as *Jepthah*'s was, in the *Spirit* of *Joy* and *Gratitude*. And besides, he meant his as a *Duty*, and as an *acceptable Service* to God—but the Vows and Resolutions of these Days *seldom* have a *good* Tendency: They are for the most Part founded on *Pique* and *Resentment*; and even upon a Supposition that we have received *Injury*—they generally take Care to bring us in *Debtor* at *last* even to the

very

very *Party* which *first* offended—A Mortification as well as an Injustice this—which must needs be very painful to a Mind the least susceptible of Friendship, or real Greatness of Disposition; insomuch that I doubt not but there are many, let their Wealth and Situation be never so great and flattering—who are now wretched, merely through a strict Observance of some idle unguarded Resolution.

In a Word—this Life necessarily affords so many and so unexpected Changes—and the Futurity even of an Hour may cause so surprizing and so striking a Vicissitude in human Affairs—that a truly wise Man will make no other Resolution—than to be as just, as honest, as friendly, as religious, and as virtuous as he can. Vows of another Kind are oftentimes vicious—at best trifling and imprudent—and always to be discountenanced, as being naturally hurtful to Religion and Virtue and social Life.

Let

Let us then endeavour to be careful of our Words as well as Works—to say and do what is most pleasing in the Sight of Heaven—as we would wish to enjoy Peace on Earth, and Peace at God's right Hand for evermore—through the Merits and Intercession of Jesus Christ our Lord—to which two sacred Persons together with the Holy Spirit be ascribed all Honour and Glory, World without End. Amen.

SERMON III.

UPON THE

GOOD SAMARITAN,

Preached at COURT,

On Sunday, October 22, 1775.

SERMON III.

LUKE x. 36, 37.

Which now of these three thinkest thou was Neighbour unto him who fell amongst the Thieves? And he said, he that shewed Mercy on him: Then said Jesus *unto him, go—and do thou likewise.*

WE are doubtless born into this World to discharge the Offices of Friendship and Society: The very first Lesson which we learn is—that (under the Providence of the Deity) we

owe

owe our Existence and Support to the Favour of others, and brought up as we *all* are in a State of Dependence—and unable to subsist alone—we see continually the Necessity which we are under of cultivating a reciprocal Kindness and good Will amongst Men. Our nearest Relations are certainly our first and strongest Bonds of Endearment; yet this Union which begins with our nearest Kindred does not end there—but extends itself far and wide, and connects us (in a certain Degree) with our Neighbours, our Country, and all Mankind.

It may be said, perhaps, that the Conduct of the Priest and Levite (as recorded in this well known Narrative before us) exceeded the Practice of the most inhuman *Christians,* those only excepted who (as Murderers) delight in Blood; and that the Part of the Samaritan would be that of Christians in general, so particularly called upon as he was. Let it be acknowledged, indeed, that the

the Case of a Traveller robbed, stripped, wounded, and, as it were, expiring for Want of some kind Friend to cloath him, and to pour Oil into his Wounds—is such, as would affect even many *very wicked* Men. How candidly therefore should we judge in this Matter of the *honest* and *benevolent* Part of Mankind? Surely there is no Doubt to be made, but that these, under the same Circumstances, would, from natural human Feelings, as well as from Principles of Christianity, discover a Sympathy, and relieve with Compassion and Care, equal to what the Samaritan shewed. Bad as the World is, we are not wanting in Thousands of Instances, wherein the Samaritan has been fully equalled.

I cannot, it is true, avoid remarking, that there are to be found, I am afraid, but too many, who tho' they could not carry themselves in so relentless a Manner as the Priest and Levite did; and tho' they should

should so far imitate the Samaritan, as to take a Fellow Creature, situated as the Traveller before us was, upon their own Beast to a Place which could afford him Comfort and Relief; yet I am afraid, I say, that we have but too many (even in this Christian Land) through Notions too contracted, and from a criminal Love of Money, who would leave this destitute Man, unwilling to exercise upon him the Generosity of a Samaritan in paying the *Expences* of *one Night* only, much less in speaking that most liberal and humane Language which the Samaritan delivered in the Morning to the Master of the House when he was obliged to leave the poor wounded Man: " Take Care "of him, and whatsoever thou spendest more, "when I come again I will repay thee." Hence we may learn, that the truly good Man, or he who wishes to imitate the good Samaritan, must exercise his Mercy (according to his Opportunities and Abilities) as well

well, when *Expences attend* such Acts of Mercy, as when *they do not*.

But we have before observed, that no *Christians* could act the Part of the Priest and Levite—those only excepted, who (as Murderers) delight in Blood: And I really believe and hope that this Observation will stand good. Still, tho' *Christians* would not suffer their Bigotry and Prejudices thus far to get the better of their natural Feelings even as *Men*, much more of their *indispensible* Duty as *Christians*; yet every Denomination amongst us have Bigotry and Prejudices too weak and even too criminal, to render the Behaviour of the Priest and Levite wholly inapplicable to ourselves. Every Nation, and every religious Profession amongst us—have hereditary Notions and contracted Opinions, which border but too much upon the Presumption and Ignorance and Obstinacy, always so conspicuous in the *Jewish* Heart. It was doubtless the

Design

Design and Employment of our Divine Lord and Master to rectify all Disorders — to remove every little narrow Prejudice which Humanity was prone to: For which Purpose he practised in his own Life — a Scheme of Benevolence as extensive as the Globe: " This *universal* Benevolence our Lord " makes the *Perfection* of *Religion*, and " the *Perfection* of *Religion* must needs be " the *Perfection* of *human Nature*."

Should indeed two Objects (equally circumstanced in Danger and Distress) present themselves to our Mercy — the one a *good* — the other a *bad* Man; or the one our *Friend* or *Acquaintance* — the other our *Enemy* or *no Acquaintance*; (if Ability be not afforded us to assist both) it seems to be the Voice of Justice as well as of Nature, and by no Means contrary to a Spirit of *universal* Benevolence — that we (in this Case) bestow our Succour and Assistance upon the *good* Man, or upon him whom we call our *Friend* or *Acquaintance*. We may, and ought to *wish* the

the other *well*; and if we do this, we act, I think, quite *equal* to the Samaritan. But when no such *Choice* of miserable Objects is presented to our Mercy, and where no such *Comparison* of Characters or Connections can be made (as was the Case with the Samaritan respecting the poor wounded Traveller) our Business is not to regard the Country—the Religion—the Connections, or even the *Character* and *Morals* of the Object (supposing that his Wants are *urgent*, and the *Danger* of his Life *apparent*, as was also manifestly the Situation of this Traveller) but in Earnest, and without Hesitation, hasten as the Samaritan did—to administer every Relief in our Power which may be necessary to the Ease and Recovery of this Object of Compassion—whether known or unknown—our Friend or Enemy—a Jew, a Turk—or even an Infidel.

We shall do well to observe further, that no Station, however opulent or dignified, is

exempt

exempt from Danger and Diſtreſs. We none of us know what a Day may bring forth, and our Misfortunes *oftentimes* ariſe where we *leaſt expected* them. The Caſe of the poor Traveller in the Goſpel may become in a great Meaſure the Caſe of the moſt independent amongſt us. If ſo, what would the Dignity, or Fortune, or Friends of ſuch an one *elſewhere* afford him? Unleſs ſome kind Samaritan ſhould happen to paſs by, he muſt (equally with the pooreſt Man) lie upon the Road weltering in his Blood, and periſh and die alone. Reflect then that ſhould *our own* Situation *require* it, how freely *we* ſhould *receive* Mercy; and ſuch a Reflection ſhould forcibly inſtruct us, that ſhould the Situation *of others* ſtand in *Need* of Mercy—we ought (if in our Power) as freely to *beſtow* it. The very Notion that Man was made after the Image of God teaches that every Individual thus afflicted has a Right to be thus humanely dealt by;

and

and when this is not the Case " Contempt " is shewed both to the *Image* and to the " *divine Original.*"

But whilst we thus insist that Humanity obliges us to assist our Brethren in their *extreme* Necessities—let it not be supposed that the great Precept of *Christian Charity* is *rigorous* but in this Case *only:* Besides those *extreme* Necessities, there are *Necessities grievous* and more *frequent*. I am unwilling to believe that there are any amongst the Rich so void of Pity as to see a fellow Creature perish before their Eyes—to see him reduced to the *last Distress*, and just ready to *expire*—without taking Pains to preserve Life in him, and to relieve him from such *Extremity;* And let me remark also—that it is a very rare Sight to behold amongst the Poor any one in a Situation *altogether* so *miserable* and *despairing*. We may therefore safely conclude that it is our Duty not only to attend to those *extraordinary* Necessities, but

but likewise—to *others* which are more *common* and *familiar* to us: For the Christian who forms a Resolution never to do good but in the *last* Necessities of the Poor—shews a Disposition in a most essential Point criminal, and directly opposite to the divine Law.

Again; *partial* Regards and *partial* Friendships may possibly become very faulty Errors. Let it be allowed thus far, that some are more linked to us as Brethren, and some of Necessity render themselves more endearing to us, than others; and Friendships of this Kind properly founded and properly conducted—bring with them great Sweets, and are productive of much real Virtue: Yet as God is the Father, and the *Jerusalem above* the Mother of us *all*—as we are all born of the same incorruptible Seed, and capable of being equal Partakers of the same divine Nature——as every Day makes some Separation amongst us, and as a few Years muſt make a total one—how reaſonable the Duty, how tender the Requeſt, that our Benevolence towards each other be extenſive—if poſſible, that it be univerſal! And tho' ſome ſhould prove unworthy of our Regard and Aſſiſtance, yet we may be aſſured that our Part is (agreeably to the Goodneſs of it) accepted with God. And indeed if we would wiſh to go and do as the wiſe Samaritan did, and as the Lawyer was commanded in the Text, we muſt effectually deſire the Good and Happineſs of the *whole* World, and do all in our Power *really* to promote it: We muſt be compaſſionate and friendly, not only in *Thought* and in *Word*, but as we have Opportunity—in *Deed* and in *Truth*: By Virtue of which godlike Diſpoſition, there will exiſt in us an Heart felt Sympathy, which will ſhew itſelf by rejoicing with thoſe that do rejoice, and mourning with them that mourn. This, in a Word, is that well inſtructed inftructed Character which completeth all Things: The Chriftian Faith may fupport, and other chriftian Virtues may defend us during our earthly Pilgrimage — but this Conduct which fo much refembles that of the good Samaritan — is what muft *finally perfect* us, and is therefore the beft adorned Pledge and Reprefentation of eternal Glory.

SERMON

SERMON IV.

UPON

A PROPER and an IMPROPER CONFORMITY
to the WORLD.

PREACHED AT
QUEEN-STREET CHAPEL,
on SUNDAY, NOVEMBER 12, 1775.

SERMON IV.

PROV. xxix. 25.

The Fear of Man bringeth a Snare.

IT muſt be allowed (with Solomon) that there is a Fear of Man which bringeth a Snare or Diſgrace; but it ſeems to be equally clear and certain that there is a Fear of Man alſo which does *not* bring a Snare or Diſgrace with it, but Honour and Happineſs. Now it will be proper to prove this, before we enlarge upon the Text; before indeed we can ſay any Thing in perfect Favour of the Proverb which it contains.

A Defire to be fpoken well of by the World in *general*—is both natural and laudable; therefore all *honourable* Methods to obtain *this* good Opinion are to be adopted and encouraged. Although the good Man, and the Man of Integrity is convinced that he has not deferved either public or private Cenfure; ftill, he cannot, fhould not always be without the *Fear* of it: Becaufe this *prudent* Fear will teach him conftantly to endeavour to keep off Slander from the *profeffed* Backbiter, and to prevent harfh Speeches falling from the Lips of thofe, who from a *weak* Head, and a Propenfity to much *idle* Talking, are apt to caufe great Mifchief to their Friends and Acquaintance, as well as to Society in general. Unjuft Cenfures can never make an *innocent* Man *truly* miferable; yet they are, doubtlefs, a very *confiderable* Abatement to his *temporal* Happinefs.

SERMON IV.

To comply seasonably, and in Proportion to their Consequence, with the *innocent* Customs and Fashions of the World—is *also*, I think, highly commendable. Wholly to give up ourselves to them—must be a *faulty Compliance*; and wholly to despise them—must be a *faulty Singularity*. The Infirmities of human Nature, and the Difficulties of human Life—seem strongly to apologize for the World, in contriving and encouraging certain Pleasures and Amusements—intended merely as seasonable, indeed *necessary* Reliefs to Care and Solitude. This Indulgence, (as we have before hinted) must have its *Bounds*, to render it either lawful or becoming; but, surely, when exercised with Prudence and Discretion—the best of Men will do right even to *countenance* such occasional Intermissions, whether of *fancied* or *real* Joys—thus authorized by the *World* and their own *Innocence*.

But let us now attend to still higher Injunctions in Favour of a *proper Conformity* to the World, or of a *laudable Fear* of Man. Masters, Parents, Princes, are to be *feared* or reverenced; and so is every Person (in a proportionable Degree) by those to whom he is *superiour*, or over whom he has any *just* and *lawful* Authority. However disgracefully such *Superiours* may fill their respective Characters—still it will be dutiful and prudent in every connected or dependent *Inferiour* to do *his* Part—to shew *Honour* to their *Stations*, though he might *justly* censure and condemn—the Men.

But if we suppose a becoming Fear or Reverence to be wanting in a Servant towards a *good* Master; how criminal the Ingratitude of *such* a Servant! And what are the Mischiefs which may not arise from *such* undutiful Conduct? If we suppose *this* Fear or Reverence to be wanting in a Child towards a *good* Parent; what is there that

is

is shameful which we may not expect from *such* a Child? Or what of Unhappiness which *such* a Parent may not tenderly experience? If we suppose this Fear or Reverence to be wanting in a Subject towards a *good* Prince; it becomes a hurtful, a destructive Principle indeed. And lastly, if we suppose *this* Fear or Reverence to be wanting towards a *good* Magistrate, or towards a *deserving* Superiour of any Kind; *that* wise *Distinction* of Station and Power so necessary to the well-being of Society — is hereby in Danger of being unhappily converted into *criminal* Discord and Confusion: In Time — the Fear of *God*, together with the *just* and *lawful* Fear of *Man*, will become equally exploded; and Men will act as if (literally speaking) they neither feared *them* who can *legally* kill the *Body only*, nor *him* who is able to destroy *both Body and Soul* in Hell. I wish indeed that the Period of Time may not be already arrived, when the *moral* Ties

without

without the *legal* would lay but *little* Restraint upon the *Generality* of Mankind. Nay, can even Laws be formed *close enough* to repel the bold Assailants of our Rights and Happiness? Or do such Offenders in in *general* discover the *least* Sense of *Shame* or *Fear* — tho' compelled to undergo all the Pain and Ignominy, which the severest Sentence (within the Power of the Laws) can pronounce against them.

I must here repeat the melancholy Supposition — that the sacred Ties of Religion *alone* — would lay but *little* Restraint upon the Generality of Mankind! Happy, however, is that Man who conforms to the *excepted Few* — who thinks with *them*, that if the Christian Religion be of the *least* Importance, it is, doubtless, of the *greatest* — that if it be *any Thing at all*, it is certainly the *one Thing especially needful*. And thrice happy that Parent, or Master of a Family, who in this Respect both *feareth* and *imitateth* pious *Joshua*; who like him thus dareth to determine: *If it seem evil unto*

SERMON IV.

unto the irreligious Multitude so to do; yet as for me and my House—we will serve the Lord.

But let me hasten now to a Vindication of the Saying of *Solomon*—that the Fear of Man bringeth a Snare.

Altho' we have been so strongly recommending a proper Conformity to the World, as in Things of manifest Importance, so likewise in Things, which, tho' in Reality trifling, Custom and even Religion itself may (in a great Measure) authorize and recommend; yet if we pursue this Conformity to the World as an *ultimate* Part of our Duty and Happiness—our Conduct becomes defective in it's *main Spring*, and our Innocence, with our Happiness, is in certain Danger of being *finally* lost. As there is a Power *above* Man, so *that* Power should always be feared and reverenced in *Preference* to Man. Whenever the Commands of the *World* oppose the Commands of *God*; I should hope ever to sacrifice the *World* (and the Power and Happiness of a *thousand fand such Worlds)* to my *superiour* Attachments to my *God*, and to *that Life and Immortality* so manifestly brought to Light by the Gospel of his blessed Son.

And yet how many has a criminal Fear of Men or of the World prevailed upon to ridicule sacred Truths! But if to be impious is to be *fashionable*; who in his Senses will dare to *comply* with the *World*, in a Matter so affronting to his God and Saviour—so degrading to the human Nature—and withal so dangerous to his own eternal Safety?

Again, with Respect to Morals also—how many have been weak and sinful enough to plead *Fashion* or *Persuasion* in Favour of Fraud, Oppression, Perjury, and indeed Vice in general. But, surely, to commit evil to *oblige others*—must be always making *that* Evil—*our own*; and to commit Evil because *others commit* it—is to make *ourselves*—*equally* guilty and responsible. *Few* Men (if *any*) have it in their Power, I fear, *wholly* to avoid the Contagion of the World

where

where the *private* Vices are *concerned:* But *all* Men have it in their Power *wholly* to avoid *this Contagion of the World* where the *public* Vices are *concerned*. If we may not always be able to refrain from doing Injury to *ourselves*; yet *no* Temptation (either of *Inclination* or *Perſuaſion*) can poſſibly juſtify us in doing Injury to *others:* In the former Caſe, *Principle may exiſt* even with *Guilt*; but in the latter, it *cannot:* Yet rather than *forfeit*—*real* Principle—every good and honeſt Man would *forfeit*—his *earthly all*.

But methinks I hear Flattery particularly vindicated—that it does not amount to a *Vice*, but is (at moſt) only a *faſhionable*, indeed a *neceſſary*—*Error*. If it be *faſhionable*, yet never let us ſink the human Underſtanding ſo low as to account it *neceſſary*. There is the greateſt Difference between Reſpect and Flattery: The one *may* be a Duty—the other *muſt* be a Fault. Rudely or unſeaſonably to tell Men of their
                                                    Imperfections

Imperfections will ever deserve Rebuke—but to ascribe to Men Virtues or Merit which we know that they are not possessed of—is as mean as it is criminal. But however Flattery may *sometimes* serve a *present* Purpose; yet upon the *whole* it seldom answers: Men who are *pleased* with it—*to Day*—may be *justly digusted* at it—*to-Morrow*; and Men who exercise it with Success *to Day*—may be *justly degraded* for it—*to Morrow*: Whether therefore Flattery be a *Vice* or an *Error only*—we may venture to pronounce *Sincerity* to be the *chief Glory* of every Man's Character—and the *Want of it* our greatest *Shame* and *Dishonour*; as we shall hope more fully to make appear in two subsequent Discourses.

As a Conclusion of the Subject before us—let it be acknowledged that the Practice of *all* Vice and Error, whether of a *public* or *private* Nature—whether done to please *ourselves* or *others*—is generally seen (sooner or later) to bring a *Snare* with it: May none of of us ever experience *this* in *both* Worlds! To speak, however, nearly in the Words of the amiable Dr. *Rogers*—after we have used our utmost Precaution—after we have called in every imaginable Assistance—great is the Work of qualifying ourselves for Heaven, and for the Characters of Saints. Let then neither the *Customs* of Mankind nor our own *self-corrupted* Hearts—let neither Profit, Pleasure, nor *Fear*, so far bias our Judgments, as to make us court the Honours or the Company—flatter the Foibles—or commend the Vices and Infidelity—of wicked and prophane Men. Religion and it's exalted List of Virtues—Heaven and all it's glorious Pretensions—are Things of *too great* Value—either to be parted with —in a *Compliment*—or sacrificed to an *impious* and *dissolute World.*

SERMON

КОНЕЦ

SERMON V.

UPON

PRAYER — what it is, and what it is not.

Preached before the UNIVERSITY of CAMBRIDGE, 1773.

SERMON V.

PSALM V. 3.

I will *direct* my Prayer unto *Thee*.

PRAYER has ever been considered in all Ages and by all Nations however barbarous and unenlightened—as a Duty becoming—*incumbent upon* Man. Not the Necessity nor Importance of Prayer then—but the *Manner* in which it *ought* to be *performed*—is intended for the Subject of our present Reflection; which seems to be happily suggested to us in the Language of the Text: " I will *direct* my Prayer unto *Thee*."

That human Nature is capable of attending so long or so steadily to *invisible* as it is to *visible* Objects—all Philosophers deny. God therefore (the Object of our Devotion) being an invisible Object—even the most pious Men find some Difficulty entirely to bring the Mind over from attending to the Things which are seen—to such a Direction of itself to the Deity, as is required in the great Duty of Prayer. Yet this very Cause of natural Wandering or Inattention in Prayer—marks out a natural Relief, tho' not, at all Times, an absolute Cure for it. It is beyond Dispute, that great Degrees of Perfection in the Act of Prayer are in our Power of attaining—if we could but be convinced of the Method of performing it aright—and secure Faith and Inclination in it's Favour.

And here I am sorry to find myself (in Justice to my Subject) under the Necessity of introducing a Variety of Observations—
the

the Truth of which will, I truſt, ſufficiently apologize for the *ſeeming* Freedom with which they may be delivered.

" The Countenance of true Devotion tho'
" not to confiſt of any hypocritical Marks
" —is, neverthelefs, peculiar to itſelf, and
" generally to be diſtinguiſhed from the
" carelefs Worſhipper." I mean to paſs over private Devotion, and only to ſpeak of the Church. But if we look around our Churches; by how few does the Deity ſeem to be *truly* worſhipped? Few even amongſt the religious Part of our Congregations appear to have a juſt Idea of the Properties of Prayer. They fancy that they have been praying, when in Fact they may not have offered up a ſingle Petition: They are apt, I fear, to miſtake Meditation for Prayer—and *thinking* only of their Sins for *confeſſing* them. Now nothing can conſtitute a *real* Confeſſion of Sins, but a deep Contrition of the Spirit; and nothing can

constitute *real* Prayer but a *Direction* of the *Soul* to the divine Object of it. The Error of *good* Men in this Matter is more to be lamented as a Misfortune than as a Crime; yet for their own Happiness as well as for the Honour of public Worship—how much is it to be wished that they would find out and rectify so general a Mistake! But what Excuse can we make for those of our Congregation, who seem to be entirely lost to all Sense of Prayer; as if they were not at all concerned in what was doing, nor even desirous of becoming so? Again, what must we think of those who hope to pass for Devotionists, and to partake of the Benefits of public Worship—merely from the Assistance and Efficacy of the Word—*Amen?* " The Prayer offered up by
" the Minister becomes the undoubted Prayer
" of the Man, who with a *Direction* of his
" *Heart to God* attends in every Part of it,
" and at the End delivers his own, *So be it:*
" But

"But what can be the Efficacy of *that* Man's "*Amen*, who speaks it only from a Kind of "*mechanical Listen* to the Voice of the Minis- "ter at the Close of a Prayer or Collect"— when he himself, perhaps, during the deli- vering of such Prayer or Collect—has been engaged—either in telling his Gold—in envying or supplanting his Neighbour—in cherishing some sinful Passion—else (which is to make the best of it) in an idle *Vacancy* of Thought?

Such is the Charge which the Clergy in too many Instances may justly lay to the People: A Charge too of a serious and af- fronting Nature. But have the People no Cause to complain of the Clergy in this Matter? Not that such a Complaint, how- ever great or just, can lessen *their* Guilt, or excuse *their* Irreverence towards God. Yet surely if *we* can with *Truth* be arraigned of *general* Negligence and Inattention in Prayer —our *own* Guilt and Irreverence towards God

God should strike us with Concern and Remorse. And I am afraid that upon true Speculation we shall find—that we have really lessened ourselves *more*, and have given greater Advantages to our *dissenting* Brethren, by these Means, than by any other whatever. Their Objections to our Liturgy (great as they originally were and still may be) seem to be manifestly exceeded by their Objections to the *Manner*, in which it is but too *generally* performed. This Opinion I gained some Years ago from the Mouth of one of their most eminent Divines; and I am concerned to add that my own Experience, since that Time, has too fully convinced me of the Justness of his Remark. We should ever remember that *merely* to *read* a Form of Prayer cannot be *praying* in the Clergy, any more than sinking into a *mere Formality* of Posture and responding can *be praying* in the People. The Articles of our Faith and our Mode of
Church-

Church-Government—we shall, I hope, be always able to *defend;* but an irreverent Method of performing Divine Service—is (doubtless) *altogether indefensible.* Do we boast of the *singular* Blessing of a *Form* of Prayer solemnly *adapted* to the *divine* Ear? The greater our Boast, the greater surely is our Reproach: And was such *Form* even *more* perfect than it is—even *more* solemnly adapted to the divine Ear; yet if in the Use or Performance of it, we should be *wilfully* deficient in that Attention—that *Direction* of the Soul which alone can constitute *true* Devotion—however we might admire it as a *Composition;* it's Beauties would soon become too familiar to us—and for Want of *Inclination* to perform the Service—we should be as ready *then* as some of us may be *now*—to cry out—" the *Church* does *indeed* " take up *too much* of our *Time* in *Prayer.*"

I wish

I wish that it may not be considered as a Misfortune, that the *dignified* amongst us should so *universally* confine themselves to *preaching*, and that the still *more important* Services of the Desk should be the *constant* Lot of the *inferiour* Clergy. This Custom (tho' exercised with great Reason in the early Parts of the Reformation) has proved, perhaps, of no *small* Disservice to public Worship—no *slender* Weapon of Defence to our *Liturgical* Adversaries: It has, perhaps, been innocently instrumental towards *raising Preaching* (let me be justified in the Expression) *above itself*, by *sinking Prayer— infinitely below itself*—towards making too many of us (for the Sake of *superiour* Fame and *superiour* Dignity, and fearless *now* of the *unmeaning* Terms—*Heresy* and *Schism)* become *extravagant Enthusiasts* (I had almost said *Mountebanks*) in the *Pulpit*, and *irreverent*—*insensible Drones* in the *Desk*. Far be it from me to degrade *rational,* nay

frequent

frequent preaching: It is a *noble and important Ordinance of the Church*, and cannot be censured but in a comparative View; as it appears to render us *wilfully* and *habitually* negligent in an *Ordinance still more noble, still more important:* And if this should be found to be in *Reality* the Case; might we not with Reason complain that we have *too much of preaching* instead of *praying*—and contend, that if any Part of the *full* Service upon a *Sunday* Morning is *ever* to be *dispensed* with— let it be—the *Sermon*.

And pardon me for suggesting that this Negligence and Inattention in the Desk, so *generally*, and, I fear, so *justly* laid to our Charge—has *somewhat* of a Foundation even *earlier* than the Period of taking *holy Orders*. I will not, I need not explain myself any further. Advice in this Matter would come with more Gracefulness from an older and a wiser Man; yet *Principiis obsta* we *all* know to be most excellent Admonition: We shall

find

find it so, respecting every *faulty* Step throughout the *whole* Journey of Life, and *especially serviceable* towards preventing a Custom or Habit in the Performance of religious Offices, which must needs reflect Dishonour upon ourselves and our Profession. Whatever our Errors may be *out* of the Church; yet I should hope that no one would wish to increase them *in* it. Our Passions, our Temptations, our Company, may, possibly, plead somewhat in our Favour for Transgressions *out* of the *Church* — but our Understandings as well as our Hearts must represent us as *wholly unpardonable* for any conscious or habitual Irreverence *within it's* sacred Walls.

If it should be conjectured, that in this Sermon I have had a *partial* Reverence to a *certain modern* Controversy; I will beg Leave to observe, that altho' too *strict* an *Adherence* to *Tradition* was complained of by our Saviour in the

Jewish

Jewish Elders—yet that the *faulty Love* of *Novelty* in the *Athenian* seems to be as sharply reprehended by St. *Paul.* Antiquity, *(merely as such)* must never be considered by *Protestants* as the *Standard* of Religion: Neither must *Antiquity (because such)* be *necessarily objected to*, and *given up* at Random, in Compliment to every *new* religious System: At this Rate of Discretion (to speak in the Words of one, who made a Study of the human Heart) " We may at Length grow weary
" of the plain Truths of the Gospel—such
" as Death and Judgement—Heaven and
" Hell; and so (even before we are aware
" of it) turn universal Sceptics, and throw
" up every Thing that is worthy of the
" Name of Religion."

To revert, however, more immediately to the Point in Question; we know that in our Liturgy as it *now* stands—God is capable of being *greatly glorified*; and let us us suppose that had it undergone an Alteration *He* would have been *equally so*: Yet since this our Form of Prayer is not likely to undergo any Alteration — it seems to be both prudent and our *Duty* to hope that *no such Alteration* was at all *necessary* — and to endeavour to supply the *seeming* Defects of it, by an *additional Zeal and Propriety* in the *Use* or *Performance* of it. An Experiment of this Sort will unavoidably be *some Relief* to the *present Complaint* — it will also greatly raise us in the Character of Devotionists — and in Time may, probably, *alter* — *possibly, amend* our Judgments as Critics; in softening what we may *now* call — a *tedious Prolixity* — into an *interesting Copiousness*; or an *heavy* and *useless Tautology* — into a *pious* and *profitable Repetition*. Be this, however, as it may; what I have been *now* contending for — is a *Sincerity of Soul* in the Act of *Prayer* — a Sincerity which shall in nowise

lose

lose it's Reward; in nowise lose it here upon Earth — in the Approbation of the Heart; in nowise lose it in Eternity — in the personal Approbation of our God.

SERMON VI.

ON

SOLOMON's REQUEST.

Preached at St. MARY LE BOW,
on SUNDAY, APRIL 20, 1771.

SERMON VI.

1 KINGS iii. 10.

And the Speech pleased the Lord that Solomon *had asked this Thing.*

SOLOMON was *now* in the Beginning of his Reign, having but in the former Chapter buried his Father King *David*. At the fifth Verse of the present Chapter we read that in *Gibeon* the Lord appeared to *Solomon* in a Dream by Night—and God said, " Ask what I shall give Thee.". We are not to judge of the *Visions* of those Days by the *Dreams* of our own; because

then

then it was very usual for the Lord to make Discoveries to the Mind when the Senses were asleep and inactive. And indeed that God does this *sometimes* even to *Us*, (tho' in a less important Way) I am very ready to believe: To say that He cannot—would be impious; to say that He has never done it—would, I suppose, be contradicting the certain Experience of many in every Age of the World. But to confine ourselves to *Solomon*, whose Mind seems to have been quite as full of *regular* Thought at the Time of this Vision—as we might have expected that it would have been, had not the Senses been locked up in Sleep: We find no rambling Answer returned to the Lord; but such an one as shewed the greatest Power of accurate and consistent speaking, as well as a most striking Diffidence, and Sublimity of Sentiment. And the Speech, we find, pleased the Lord. It could not do otherwise. Picture to yourselves

selves so *young* a Man succeeding to the Crown of so *vast* a Kingdom: Think too of the natural Gaiety of *Solomon*'s Temper; and then let us wondering—revere him for his Choice, in asking only for Wisdom and Understanding, by which he might discern between good and Evil, and so judge his People righteously.

And here let me refer you to the liberal reply on God's Part. No Wonder that a Promise so much exceeding the Request—caused the rapturous Heart of *Solomon* to wipe the drowsy Slumbers from his Eyes, and every other Sense to arise into peculiar Activity. Yes, he awoke, and behold it was a Dream: Yet not doubting the Reality of the heavenly Vision, " he came to " *Jerusalem*, and stood before the Ark of " the Covenant of the Lord, and offered " up Burnt-Offerings, and Peace-Offerings."

Now as a Trial of his Wisdom and righteous Judgment—there came two Wo-

men before him, bringing with them a *dead* and a *living* Child. The Conteſt before the King was— whoſe the *living* Child ſhould be—each declaring that it was hers. *Solomon*'s Method of ſearching out the Mother was every Thing that is juſt, wonderful, and affecting. Juſt indeed it could not well be to have taken away the Life of the innocent Babe: Yet as we are to ſuppoſe that *Solomon* knew how human Nature would work in this Matter—he in Appearance forgets that the Thing claimed had a *Being* valuable even to thoſe who claimed it; and therefore by ordering the Child to be divided, he ſuppoſes that he might pleaſe them both, and be thought by the Court to have paſſed a righteous Judgment. It may not be uninteresting, perhaps, to fancy this Scene now before us. *Solomon* upon his Throne—the Sword drawn in his Hand—and the poor little Innocent upon the Point of being ſacrificed. Behold the
real

real Mother fwooning, as it were, at the Sight of the drawn Sword, juft ready to fall upon, nay and to divide her Infant! How do her maternal Bowels *yearn* upon the little Victim—to fave whom (tho' it be delivered up to a pretended Parent) mark her generous Refignation: "O my Lord—give "*her* the *living* Child, and in no wife flay "it." Upon which, fancy the other *(unnatural)* Woman (lofing all Regard for the Babe, and filled with Revenge towards the agitated, humane Mother) exulting at the Sentence of the Judge, and anxious for the Execution of it—hear her own barbarous Expreffion—let it be neither *mine* nor *thine*, but *divide* it. Then did the King's Difcernment appear juft both to himfelf and to thofe prefent. The Difference of Countenance and Behaviour in the two Women—plainly pointed out the *real* Mother of the Child: And the King anfwered and faid—"Give *her* the *living* Child"—

"ber who asked it's *Life*—"and in no wise "slay it—for *she* is the *Mother* thereof. "And all *Israel* heard of the Judgment "which the King had judged, and they "feared the King, for they saw that the "Wisdom of God was in him to do Judg- "ment."

The chief Use that I would wish to make of this Promise to *Solomon* and the Fulfillment of it is—that as *he* asked of God the Blessing of a wise and understanding Heart to govern his People—so *we* should learn to apply to the same all powerful Deity for the Enjoyment of every lawful and eligible Wish. It is possible for us to thirst after Things, which tho' lawful— may not be expedient to our Happiness. Now all the Pleasures dependent upon Time or the World—are capable of being *thus* mistaken by us; and therefore altho' we should ask any of them of God, or should *wish* for them only, and he should not

permit

permit them to be given to us—yet if we search diligently we shall find, by and by, upon Reflection and Experience—that such Disappointment has been profitable to us. So likewise if we (as it were) insist upon being gratified—and God acquiesces in our random and ill-judged Petitions—Time and Circumstances in Life, will, probably, soon convince us, that our Notions of Happiness were falsly grounded; for that by the *Enjoyment* of our hasty and *positive* Wishes—we are become *wretched*. Where shall we meet with the Man, who in some *material* Instance or another—has not experienced the Truth of these Observations?

With Regard indeed to Blessings which owe not their Existence or Support to the Changes and Chances of this mortal Life—for Blessings like these we cannot be too importunate. It never can be wrong to beseech the Almighty to make us honest, humane,

humane, juſt, and good. We may reſt aſſured that it never can be againſt the divine Will—that Mankind ſhould be poſſeſſed of Virtues like theſe: On the Contrary, that he is ever moſtly delighted with thoſe Diſpoſitions, in whom theſe Virtues are moſtly to be found. The more averſe we are by Nature from the Practice of what is right—the more importunate ſhould our Requeſts be. *Solomon*, it is true, received as ſoon as he aſked: Yet at the Time that we admire the Power and extraordinary Favour of the Deity reſpecting *Solomon*—let us take Care that we diſtruſt him not reſpecting *ourſelves*; tho' *we* ſeek *our* ſpiritual Bleſſings with Sighs and Tears—and tho' *we* wait *long* for *Enjoyment*. Never let us deſpair—never let us give over petitioning the Almighty for any Thing which tends to *his* Glory, and the good of the Chriſtian and moral World. Altho' Days of immediate Inſpiration as well as heavenly Viſions
—are

—are *now* Things not to be expected; yet what happened to our Forefathers should be sufficient to fix in *us* the same Confidence in the same God: Added to all this—*we* believe and preach for *our* happy Conviction in this Point—the Omnipotent himself risen from the Dead.

As to the *exact* Nature of *Solomon*'s Request (however meritorious, and however proper for *him*) it is of Concern but to *Few*. *Few* are born to govern over a great People! Those indeed who act as Rulers in Life (tho' it be only over a private Family or a small Community of Men) will do right to join in *Solomon*'s Petition. Let it be remembered, that to *govern well* is more difficult than to be *well governed*; more difficult, I mean, with Regard to pleasing God: To wish to do this—is therefore certainly a moral Wish, and as such must be always lawful and expedient. The *Wisdom* of *Solomon*, as it is *never* to be
found

found in *any* Man, so it can *never* be *necessary* in *any* Man.—But as to a good Heart—this is *always necessary* in *every* Man, (especially in him who governs)—and it should be the Business of our Lives to obtain and to preserve it. And an understanding Heart in this Sense—to discern between good and evil—brings the Application of *Solomon* home—to Mankind in general. The Man who desires to love his God with all possible ~~Serenity~~ *sincerity* of Soul —to do to others as he would wish that they should do to *him*—and to learn and labour to do his Duty in that State of Life unto which it shall have pleased God to call him; the Man, I say, who *wishes thus* cannot be without an understanding Heart to judge and well govern himself, and such an one may rest assured, that the Speech will ever please the Lord that he asked this Thing.

And

And whilst we *thus* apply for moral or spiritual Blessings *only*—we may, probably, procure temporal Blessings *also*. Promises indeed belong to Times of Inspiration—we must not expect *them*; but it is the Property of divine Goodness to confer even *more* than we *desire*. It was but too natural to suppose that *Solomon* would have asked for Riches and Honours—or Success in War—or long Life: Yet when he confined his Request so intirely to the Mind—how gracious was the Promise on God's Part, touching every temporal Comfort and Advantage!

But let it be with great Seriousness considered—that our own *best* Endeavours are *absolutely necessary*—that our Prayers and Confidence on God will not do *alone*. As the Proof of a good Heart cannot be given without a Temptation to evil or an Opportunity of acting well; so unless we use the natural Means to keep off an Evil, and

allow

allow ourselves Time for the Practice of Good—such Proof of an understanding Heart must needs be wanting with Respect to the World, and as I should think—it must be very imperfect in the Sight of God. *Solomon* himself, tho' his Knowledge was in a great Measure infused, did not neglect to cultivate such Knowledge, thus by Application and Care perfecting the extraordinary Gifts which he had received of Heaven.

The chief Instruction, however, which the present Subject conveys to us—is manifestly confined to Petitions to the divine Throne. If then we wish for prosperous Fortune, or to escape an impending Affliction—always let us address the Deity in these Words of our resigned Saviour—" Father, if Thou art willing." This let us do, altho' we seek Prosperity with pleasing Sensations—and back our Petitions to avoid Misfortunes, with strong Crying and Tears.

Tears. But for spiritual Blessings—Blessings which intirely depend upon the Mind—for these (as we have before observed)—we cannot be too *positive* or too importunate: "The more earnestly we cry—the more lively Sense do we discover of the Worth of such Blessings, and the better Disposition to receive them." And if we find (for some wise Purposes) that God witholds from us a *Goodness of Heart*; let us persevere in asking it—even in the Words of the Patriarch *Jacob*—"I will not let Thee go, unless Thou bless me." To this divine Being, *who* is always more ready to *hear* than *we* to *pray*—and to give *more* than we desire or deserve—to Him (the Father, Son, and Holy Ghost) be everlasting Praise—even from Generation to Generation—World without End. Amen.

SERMON

SERMON VII.

UPON

AGUR's REQUEST.

SERMON VII.

Preached at COURT on *Sunday, Oct.* 2, 1774.

PROVERBS XXX. 7, 8, 9.

Two Things have I required of Thee, deny me them not, before I die: Remove far from me Vanity and Lies; give me neither Riches nor Poverty; feed me with Food convenient for me: Left I be full and deny Thee, and say who is the Lord? or left I be poor and steal, and take the Name of my God in vain.

FROM the Text we are invited to draw the two Extremes—*Greatness* and *Obscurity*—of Station—*Riches*, and *Poverty*: Afterwards, the *Medium* of these,

these, which according to wise *Agur* is the *Standard* of human Happiness. But I shall, finally, have Occasion to observe, that only the Nature of Things is here to be attended to, which Men may either improve or vitiate, as they are influenced by their Passions and Conduct.

"Prosperity then considered in the *best* Light is accompanied with many Inconveniencies—considered in *any other* Light—it is, doubtless, a dangerous State." The profuse, giddy, dissipating Man of Fortune has ever round him a thousand servile Parasites—a thousand fawning Sycophants—ready to immortalize his few and, perhaps, but *little* Virtues; or if he be even devoid of *any* Virtues—to construe into *Virtues*, the most glaring *Vices*. His Life, in short, is a continued Delusion; and when he comes to die, it is well for him if he does not experience, that he has not only been flattered out of his *Fortune*, but out of his *Happiness also*.

Again,

Again, in our Acquisition of Riches and Honours—we too generally neglect to sacrifice to Contentment, the chief Spring of human Happiness. " Some of this Stamp " are governed by the *Clue* of Ambition, " others by the *Lure* of Avarice." Ambition when it excites a Man to just and honourable Actions upon just and honourable Principles—such as make him grateful for his present Situation, tho' willing to raise it—such as render him delighted with no Popularity but what is seconded by the *Testimony* of his *own Heart*; this Man's Ambition is laudable, and must afford him real Satisfaction: But we are now speaking of a Passion which prevails upon a Man to go into the World mindful of himself only; " who catches at the Applause of an " idle, impetuous, mistaken Multitude, " without once caring whether he has de- " served it or not—or what Use he should " put it to." Now such an one is necessarily *disquieted* both in his *Successes* and in his *Disappointments*: If Hundreds attend upon him to proclaim his Greatness—his Vanity wishes for Thousands—and if Thousands—then for Tens of Thousands—and so on, till the whole Earth should pay him Adoration: And even in this Case, he would be more apt with *Alexander* to wish for *other* Worlds which may afford his Vanity *fresh* Qualifications—than with the *satisfied Domitian* (after he had possessed himself of the *Roman* Empire) to turn his Desires upon *catching Flies*. But should the Man of this Turn be disappointed in his Hopes and Expectations—totally unsuccessful in any of his *favourite* Schemes—he henceforth leads a Life of Discouragement, and if I may so say—of *proud* Despair.

Next let us take a faint Survey of the Miser, and see how far his Condition is to be *envied*—or rather *dreaded*. Avarice is
said

said to stick deeper into the Soul than any other Vice; and indeed very little of Obfervation will convince us of the Truth of this: In general, Avarice strikes at the Root of every Thing great and becoming: It's Poffeffor (according to Mr. *Addifon*) is neither happy *himfelf*, nor will he let thofe *connected with him* be fo: His Character is feldom other, than that of a peevifh and cruel *Mafter*—a fevere *Parent*—a gloomy, unaffectionate *Hufband*—a referved and a fufpecting *Friend*. Surely Avarice is a *fingular* Curfe upon whomfoever it falls: For notwithftanding every Argument in Favour of prudent Gain and prudent Management —the Opinion of a Mifer debafes the very Being of a human Creature, " and caufes " our valuable Paffions, which might other- " wife have made us happy, to leave their " natural Bent, and expofe us to the Hatred " of God and the World."

But to shift this Scene, and to suppose Wealth and Honours to exist without Avarice and Discontent: Still how naturally do these Situations lead Men on to Noise and Hurry, and a continued Round of idle Dissipation. What great Command must these Men have over themselves—to give the Mind *Leisure* to think *seriously*; and how apt their Situations in Life are to make them so sensible of being able to help *themselves*, as to *forget*, or even, I fear, sometimes, to *disown* the *All-sufficiency* of God —or in the Words of *Agur*—to be full and deny Him, and say, who is the Lord?

To wish then for any of these Characters (if such be the Effects of them) would be Folly, and hurtful to us, who have all the Reason in the World to wish to be removed far from them. Nor, as I am now to observe—will *extreme* Poverty or extreme Obscurity of Station be found *desirable*, or indeed, generally speaking, conducive to
Religion

Religion and *Virtue*. As wretched as they are numerous are the Inconveniencies of *this* State. Even the very *Nature* of a Man may be *changed* by it. A Thousand Things happen to him which the *World* do not, or will not *know* of—cannot, or will not *prevent*. Friendship he finds but an airy Sound: The rich and goodly Produce of the Earth is nothing to *him*; *he* enjoys these Things *no more* than the *irrational* Parts of the Creation: Nay, nor *so much*—because Nourishment is dealt out to *them* agreeably to their respective Natures: He seems, in a Word, to be shut out from Society—to be denied every Privilege due to his Existence. Now what Encouragement is to be expected in such a Breast as this? Is it, can it be pleasing thus to breathe, known only to Contempt, Solitude, and Want? Is it unlikely indeed that we may be led to charge God *foolishly* when such a Scene of complicated Ills is placed

placed before us? To think that our Piety, our many humane Virtues, and withal an honest, incessant Industry—to think that all these are *sometimes* insufficient to keep us from the sad School of Poverty—must be a Reflection, which none but very great Souls can possibly support: The Chances, however, are so much against even the *best* of us, that if we have a Mind to be secure—we shall never *request* to be put to the *Trial* of it. And if this be the Case with the Man of Poverty who is willing to make every possible Resistance against the Evils so incident to his Situation; how much more dangerous must *his* Condition be, who at *once* falls into the Snare which pious *Agur* wishes to avoid—who at *once* is induced to *steal*, and to take the Name of his God in *vain?* How such a Disposition increases by Indulgence—I need not undertake to prove: The Man—who being exposed to Want *thus readily* parts with

his

his *Honesty* to gain Relief—will very soon be prevailed upon to part with his *Religion too*; and having once given up these Valuables—he finds no *Inclination*—but if an *Inclination*, he seldom has *Power* to desist from following this unjust and illegal Course, till he becomes a Sacrifice to the Laws of his Country.

Let not what I have urged against Affluence and Poverty—or against the most exalted and the most obscure Situations—be received, as if I supposed that God by placing us in *either* puts it out of our *Power* to *please* Him: We may, doubtless, and it is expected that we *shall* be *good* Servants under *any* Circumstances. What I have endeavoured to prove is—that *some* Situations require greater Fortitude, greater Perseverance than *others*—that the rich or great Man's Life is far from a *secure*, and *should* be as far from an *idle* one—that his Trust is of an important Nature, and that

he

he has the whole World to perfuade him to break and violate it. So on the other Hand, that a State of Poverty and extreme Obfcurity is alfo vaftly intricate, and dangerous to our Virtue—that the poor Man's general Fate in the World is fuch as muft hurt a rational Creature, and that unlefs he puts on the whole Armour of God, he will have an hard Matter to withftand fo fevere a Conflict. Yet if we were but to guard the Mind with Reafon and Reflection enough to make us look upon ourfelves at all Times as under the Guidance of a God, who (if we afk it with Sincerity) will give us Ability to overcome our Trials, (however great and numerous) and who (hereafter at leaft) will reward us according to the Nature and Frequency of fuch Victories; if, I fay, we can but be convinced of this moft happy Truth (which as Chriftians we are bound to believe)—*then* may we be indifferent, as it were, in our

our Choice of Situations: Or though (to avoid a greater Share of sinful Temptation, and to enjoy the less disturbed Mediocrity) we should request to be removed from Riches and Poverty—yet we shall be happy, because we shall act becomingly and as God's Servants—let either the one or the other prove our appointed Lot.

But it may be Time now to introduce the *Eligibleness* of *that State* which *Agur* so much wishes to *enjoy*—the *Happiness* of *that Man* whom *Agur* so much wishes to *be*—A Man whom Poverty does not afflict, nor Riches torment—A Man neither obnoxious to the *Envy* so peculiar to the *Great,* nor yet to the *Contempt* so often thrown upon the Man of *Poverty*—A Man who sleeps sound; undisturbed either by the Bitterness of Distress, or by the Restlessness of Luxury—A Man, who when he awakes—wants not *Means* to obtain his *daily Bread,* nor yet is filled with *trifling Care*

Care how to pass the *Day* in *expensive* Dissipation—A Man who thinks upon his God with Gratitude, and justly commends his Estate before him; which, though it forbids him the Pomp of a Monarch, amply fills up this Degree of *dangerous* Greatness, by placing him above the sad Ills of the wretched Slave—A Man, who has it not in his Power to be so lost in Sensuality and Independency—to be so full as to deny his God; nor has he any Inducement from the Feelings of Adversity, either to steal, or to take the Name of his God in vain—A Man, in a Word, who has great Reason to be pleased and happy with his Lot, which is, doubtless, cast upon the fairest Ground—where he is not " liable to be trampled upon as the humble Shrub, nor exposed to Winds like the lofty Pine."

If the *Eligibleness* of the *State* and the *Happiness* of the *Man* were always *sure* to be *thus* united; we might congratulate the

far

far greater Part of Mankind upon being happy, to whofe Lot this middle Station manifeftly falls. But this, I fear, is by no Means the Cafe. Perfons in the middle Station are too apt to behave tyrannically to their Inferiours, and infolently to their Betters; and to adopt a Mode of *Living* in Imitation of their Superiours—as aukward as it is miftaken—as abfurd and ridiculous, as it is *hurtful* to their *Fortunes* and *dangerous* to their *Reputations*. Nay, upon a ftrict Obfervance it will be found perhaps—that Men thus placed in a Situation fo calculated by Nature to render them *happieft*—are the Characters in Life who make *themfelves more* wretched, and offend Religion and Society *more* than Men placed in the *extreme* Stations—of Greatnefs and Obfcurity— of Riches and Poverty. So that after all—it is not *this* or *that* Situation, but our *well* or *ill* behaving ourfelves in our own *refpective* ones—which alone can
juftly

juſtly gain us either Eſteem or Reproach, or juſtly conſtitute us either happy or miſerable. *Happy* did I ſay? It is eaſily pronounced, and the Word carries with it a moſt delightful Sound; but it is an Epithet of ſuch a Nature, that in order to prove it's Juſtneſs, a Man muſt ſpeak it of *himſelf*. Nay, ſo ſudden and ſo great are the Changes of the human Heart—that a Man may *think* himſelf and may *be—happy—to Day*—and *think* himſelf and may *be—deſervedly wretched—to Morrow*: Therefore no *juſt* Eſtimate of human Happineſs can be taken—till we come to die. This is the only Period, when Things are likely to appear ſtripped of all Diſguiſe—the only Period when we may be ſuppoſed incapable of deceiving—either ourſelves or others: No Room being *now* left for a Change of Sentiment and Conduct—we are likelieſt to arrive at an *almoſt certain* Knowledge of *what* we *are*—*what* we *have been*—*what* we *shall be:* In order to gain this moſt important Secret—the grand Queſtion will be—not *what* Station we have *filled,* but *how* we have *filled* it? Notwithſtanding therefore the *Wiſdom* of *Agur*'s Requeſt—we ſhall do well to attend to the ſtill *wiſer* Conſideration—that the true Eſtimate of Man's Happineſs is not to be formed from *Station*—but from *Action*—Action founded upon this *great Chriſtian* Principle——that Vice in *any* Station—*muſt* be puniſhed——Virtue in *any* Station—*muſt* be rewarded.

SERMON VIII.

UPON

PLAIN TRUTH.

SERMON VIII.

MATTHEW ii. 2.

Where is he that is born King of the Jews?

TRUTH (by which I mean especially—*divine* Truth) is the *one* Thing here below—worthy of the Care and Refearches of Man. It *alone* is the Source of folid Satisfaction; the Foundation of our *Hopes*, the Confolation of our *Fears*—the Soother of our *Misfortunes*, the Remedy of all our *Pains:* It *alone* is the *Refource* of a *good* Confcience, the Ter-

ror of a *bad* one—the secret *Torture* of *Vice*, the inward *Recompence* of *Virtue:* It *alone* immortalizes those who *love* it—renders glorious the *Chains* of those who *suffer* for it—and respectable the *Poverty* of those, who have quitted *all* for it's Sake.

There are, who love to make *Truth* the Subject of the Contention of *vain* Philosophy. There are again, who wish (as it were) to know the *Truth*, but they search not for it as they *ought*, because (at the Bottom) they would be displeased to find it. And there are a third Sort of Men, who being somewhat more flexible—suffer themselves to *stagger* at the Evidence of *divine* Truth; yet repulsed by the *Difficulties* which it *proposes*, and the *Perseverance* which it *requires*—they receive it not with *that* Joy and Knowledge which it inspires, when Men have been *for some Time* acquainted with it.

How

How different *these* Dispositions to *that* of the three eastern Sages! Accustomed as they had been by a *public* Profession of Wisdom and Philosophy to have Recourse to the Powers of *vain* human Reason, and to soar above *popular* Prejudices; yet in the present Case they did not so much as *attempt* to examine if this *new* Star could not find it's *Causes* in *Nature:* Instructed by the inspired Prophets concerning this *new* Star of *Jacob*—that it *must* one Day appear—they suffer *it* at *once* to determine and to conduct them—knowing that divine *Grace* always leaves *some* Obscurities in the Ways wherein it calls us, in order that it might not take from our Faith the *Merit* of a Submission—and that when Men are so happy as to discover only one *Glimmering* of Truth, the Uprightness of the Heart should supply what is *wanting* in the Evidence of the Light: " We have seen his

"Star, say the wise Men, and are come to "worship Him."

These eastern Sages could not be ignorant that the News which they came to pronounce at *Jerusalem* would be displeasing to *Herod:* He was ever in Fear that some Heir of the Blood of the Kings of *Judah* would claim the Heritage of his Fathers, and sit upon the Throne promised to their Posterity: Upon which Account we must not wonder that he appears so little to respect Men, who declare in the Midst of *Jerusalem* that the *King* of the *Jews* is *born*, and declare him too to a People so zealous for the Blood of *David*, and so impatient of all foreign Dominion. And yet the wise Men conceal nothing of what they had seen in the East:—They do not cover this great Event over with Expressions at all calculated to suppress the Jealousy of *Herod*. They might indeed have called the *Messiah*, whom they were

seeking

seeking, the *Embassador of Heaven,* or the *Desire* of *Nations*: They might, it is true, have marked him out by Titles *even less odious* to the Ambition of *Herod:* But full of the *Truth* which had appeared to them—they know nothing of such timid Management—concluding that those who had not a Mind to receive the *Truth* but thro' the Channel of *Error*—were not *worthy* of it: They could not explain their Errand under *Reserves* and *Disguises unworthy* of it: They ask without Hesitation—where is he who is born King of the *Jews?* They do not propose their Question with a *soft Medium* likely to produce an Answer to *deceive* them—they wished to be convinced—they sought the *Truth* with *Sincerity,* and therefore it was that they so *happily found* it.

A Disposition *this,* as rare and uncommon in *Degree,* as the great Event itself, which we are *here* contemplating. Men do not find the *Truth*, becaufe they do not feek it with an Heart upright and fincere: They difperfe throughout all Points which lead to it—Clouds, which caufe them to lofe their Way: We indeed confult touching this Matter—but we cover our Paffions over with Colours fo *foft* and *fo like* unto the *Truth*, that we force ourfelves, at Length, to anfwer—that fuch *Deception*—is Truth itfelf: We have no Inclination to be *inftructed*—we wifh to be *deceived*; and to add to *the Paffion* which thus *inflaves* us—an *Authority*, which ferves only to calm and ftupify us. Such is the Illufion of, I fear, the far greater Part of Mankind! Even the beft of Men have, I fear, within them *fome* fecret and privileged Attachment, by Means of which they take but *Half* the Guide of Confcience—fome cherifhed, ill-turned Paffion (faved from the Afhes of others) which prevents them from fearching heartily for the Truth.

Again,

Again, there are always of our Neighbours and Acquaintance, whose Conduct betrays us. Our Friends are silent: Our Superiours, through Complaisance, are very careful and tender of their Sentiments: Our Inferiours are perpetually upon their Guard, lest they should offend us: The World in general indeed speak in such soothing Accents, as only serve to draw a fresh Veil over our Affliction: The Hand which should *kindly* mark out our Defects to us— so far from attempting to reclaim us—is *thus* too often used, only to stamp us with a *fresh* Blemish. Behold the contrary Conduct of the wise Men: Alone—without any Regard to their Friends and Neighbours —in Spite of all the *public* Speeches and Derisions—whilst the *Rest* of the People either despise the miraculous Star, or consider it only as the Observation and the Design of these three Sages—as an *affronting* Design, and a Weakness *unworthy* of them

them to receive and countenance.—Alone, I say, these good and wise Men declare against the common Sentiment: They alone obey the *new* Guide: They alone forsake their Country and their Children, and account as nothing impossible *that Singularity*, of which the heavenly Luminary discovers to them the *Necessity* and the *Wisdom*.

And here I am led to another Instruction well worthy of our Attention. What oftentimes causes the *Truth* to be useless even to good inclined Men is—that they do not judge of it by the Lights of their *own* Mind, but by the Impression which it makes upon *others*. In those *happy* Moments, when we *seek* not the *Truth* but in our *own particular* Conscience, we *necessarily* see our Errors, and condemn *ourselves* in the Sight of God. We *instantly* propose to ourselves a *new* Way. In a short Time after, we enter again into the World, and not consulting any longer *more* than *common* Example—we begin to *justify* ourselves—we restore to ourselves *again* that *false* Peace, which *before,* in *private,* we had endeavoured to destroy. Hence we may *also* learn, that the *Perseverance* which the Cause of *Truth* requires—makes *it* too often to become extinct within us: It affects us as it did the young Man in the Gospel—not as it did the wise Men, when on their Return Home—the miraculous Star appeared to them again.

They had seen the Magnificence of *Jerusalem*—the Pomp of it's Edifices—the Majesty of it's Temple—the Grandeur of the Court of *Herod:* But the Gospel does not remark that they were touched with this Spectacle of human Glory: They behold *all* these grand Objects without Attention—without Pleasure—without any Mark of Approbation or Surprize: They do not once ask for the Treasury, and the Riches of the Temple; being *wholly* intent

tent upon the Light from Heaven which had shewed itself to them—they had no Eyes for what passed in the World: Their Hearts being thus detached from *every* Thing else—would find out nothing but *that Truth*, which so rejoiced, which so interested, which so comforted and refreshed them.

But where shall we meet with Men, who, like these eastern Sages, after having known *the Truth*—will not henceforth look upon any Thing else but *it?* Who make *it* the Resource of all their Labours—the Spur of their Inactivity—the Succour of their Temptations—the most solid and endearing Delight of their Soul? And yet we may rest assured—that the World—that it's Pleasures—that it's Hopes—that it's Greatness—must needs appear vain, puerile, disgustful—when compared with those Pleasures, those Hopes, and that Greatness, which present themselves to the

Man

Man who knows, and is known of God—to the Man, who regards not this lower Earth, but as a Country which *must*, one Day, be totally destroyed—to the Man, whom nothing can *substantially* please, but what in it's Nature must continue to please *for ever:* Finally, all the Objects of Vanity are nothing to such a Man as *this*—but either as Embarrassments in the Way of his Duty, or sad Monuments, which force upon him the Remembrance of his Crimes.

Such are the happy Fruits of receiving *the Truth* (as the three eastern Sages did) with Submission, with Sincerity, with Joy. May *all* Mankind experience these good Effects of an honest and an undissembling Heart, if it were only that we might live quiet and *peaceable* Lives *here;* but chiefly, as an Heart devoted to *the Truth* cannot fail of rendering us happy in another and

and a better Life, through the Merits and Interceſſion of that divine Perſonage, who tho' *born King of the* Jews—came into the World, and died—for the Benefit and Salvation of all Kingdoms and Nations of the World.

SERMON IX.

UPON

TRUTH DISSEMBLED.

SERMON IX.

MATTHEW ii. 5.

And they said unto him — in Bethlehem *of Judea.*

WE are here to point out the *Deformity* of Truth — when *dissembled* in the Manner that it was by the chief Priests and Scribes — in the Answer given to *Herod* in the Text.

Consulted by *Herod* upon the Place where the *Christ* should be born — they answer to the *Truth* — that *Bethlehem* was the Place marked out by the Prophets — wherein would be accomplished this great Event: But they do not add—that the Star foretold in the inspired Books having, at Length, appeared—that the Kings of *Saba* and *Arabia* being come with Presents to adore the new-born Chief destined to rule over *Israel*—it ought to be no longer doubted but that the Clouds had *now* brought forth *this Just One:* They do not assemble the *People* together to declare to them these happy Tidings: They do not attend the wise Men to *Bethlehem,* that by these Means they might animate *Jerusalem* by their Example: Repulsed by a *criminal* Timidity they observe a total Silence respecting *these* Matters—they *retain* the Truth in *Injustice;* and whilst Strangers come from the Extremities of the East to publish aloud in *Jerusalem*—that the King of the Jews is born—these Preachers—these Elders and Scribes—say nothing about this Event, but sacrifice to the Ambition of *Herod*—the

Interests

SERMON IX.

Interests of *Truth*——the *Hope* most dear to their Nation—and the Chief Honour of all their Ministry.

But this Defect, in certain Points, is but too prevailing in private Life: Even the best of us oftentimes render ourselves culpable by this *silent* Dissimulation towards our Brethren: We are apt to think that we have discharged our Duty to Truth, so long as we say nothing *against* it: We hear Virtue *decried*, the Doctrine of the World *maintained*—*it's* Abuses and Maxims *justified*, and *those* of the Gospel *ridiculed* and *blasphemed*: We hear *all* this, I say, without submitting, perhaps, to such Impiety *ourselves*; and yet we have not Fortitude enough to disavow it *openly*, but content ourselves in not authorising it by our *own* Example. Now it appears to me *certain*:— that as we are *all* charged *individually* with the Interests of *Truth*; to be *silent* when Men *attack* it openly *before us*—is, in a

criminal

criminal Degree, to become *ourſelves*—it's *Enemy* and *Deceiver*.

There is a ſecond Manner, by which Men *diſſemble* the Truth; in *ſoftening* it with Temperaments and a Complaiſance which *affront* and wound it. The Prieſts and the Scribes *forced* by the *Evidence* of the wiſe Men to give *Glory* to the *Truth*—*ſoften* the *Authority* of it, by Expreſſions of *Reſerve*. They attempt to leſſen the *Reſpect* which they owe to the *Truth*, by a *Complaiſance* which they wiſh to ſhew to *Herod*. They ſuppreſs the Title of *King*, which the wiſe Men came to *give*, and which the Prophets had ſo often *given* —to the *Meſſiah*: They mark *Him* out by *one* Quality *only*—*Him* who had *all* Knowledge and *all* Power at his own Diſpoſal: They chuſe rather to repreſent him as a Lawgiver eſtabliſhed to rule the Manners, than as a Saviour riſen up to deliver his People from Slavery: And altho' they themſelves

selves looked for a *Messiah*—a King and Conqueror—yet they *palliate* the Truth, which they have even a Mind to *avow*—and labour to blind the Prince, whose Ear they had so firmly obtained.

In this Particular the Destiny of great Men is really deplorable. It is seldom that they are *instructed*, because it is seldom that those about them will attempt to *instruct* them, but by *pleasing* them. And yet methinks the Generality of them would love *Sincerity*, if they were but once to become *acquainted* with it. The Passions, and the Follies of the Age, assisted by all the Pleasures which naturally encompass the Dwellings of the *Great*—are able, I will allow, but too often to drag Them into Attention: But at the Bottom—I am willing to believe that *Sincerity* is *respected* by them. Such is the Fashion of the World, that *Ignorance of Truth* causes *more Princes* and *great Men* to be censured and condemned
—th in

—than Persons of the *meanest* State and Condition; and I am convinced, that *that* base Complaisance which is too generally shewed towards the *Great*, both by State and *Church* Ministers—dishonour a *Country more*, and brings *more* Odium upon *Religion*—than the most glaring Scandals and Misfortunes which afflict either the *Church* or the State.

But are Princes and great Men *only—deceived?* And are those *about* Princes and great Men the *only* Persons who *flatter* and *deceive?* Look into *private* Life, and you will find that the Conversation, the Conduct, and Behaviour of Mankind—are but too often *Palliations* of the *Truth—Temperaments* intended to reconcile *it* with the Prejudices and Passions of those with whom they live and are acquainted, or from whom they conceive Hopes and Expectations of Favours. How seldom do we shew them real Truths, but by Ways which

SERMON IX.

which we know will *pleafe* them? How ready are we to difcover a fair Side even in their moft glaring Imperfections? And as all the Paffions bear a Refemblance to fome *Virtue,* how apt is miftaken Man to feek to *know himfelf,* by the Affiftance only of *fuch Refemblance!*

Thus it happens—that in the Prefence of a *too ambitious* Man, we fpeak of the Love of Glory and of the Defire of gaining it, as the *only* Thoughts becoming a *great* Mind: We flatter his Pride—we fet Fire to his Wifhes by Hope, and by flattering and chimerical Predictions: We nourifh the Error of his Imagination, in bringing *near* to him *Phantoms,* with which he is *ever* feeding himfelf. We venture, *perhaps,* to complain in *general*—that Men fhould be *fo much* agitated about Things which *Hazard* diftributes, and which Death *to Morrow* may fnatch from us: But how *feldom* do we *venture* to blame that *foolish* Friend, who sacrifices to such a mere *Vapour*—his Repose—his Life—and his Conscience!

In the Presence of a Man given to Revenge—we are apt to justify his Resentment and his Choler: We justify his Crime in his *Spirit:* We gratify his Passion, in exaggerating the Rancour of his Enemy. We venture, perhaps, to say, that we ought to pardon one another; but how seldom do we venture to *add*—that the first Degree of a Pardon—is never more to speak of an Injury which we have received!

In the Presence of a Prodigal—his Profusions strike us only as an Air of *Generosity* and *Elegance:* Before a Miser—his hard-heartedness and sordid Soul—are nothing more than *wise* Moderation, and *good* domestic Conduct: Nay, and before the *Great* themselves—Men, whom at a *Distance,* we are so ready to find Fault with—

their

SERMON IX.

their Prejudices and *their* Errors—receive from us Apologies altogether *borrowed:* We seem to respect their Imperfections as we do their *Persons,*—and even to make *their* Prejudices become our *own.*

In short, such is the mistaken Turn of Mankind in general—that they too readily borrow the Errors of those, with whom they are connected. Few of us speak our *own* Language: And this *unworthy* Breach of *Sincerity* we call—the *Science* of the *World*—the *great* Art of *pleasing* and *prospering.*

Think not that I mean to condemn the *Temperaments* of a wise and discreet *Prudence,* which does not appear to encourage Men in their *Prejudices,* but to fix them more *firmly* in the Ways of *Rule* and *Duty.* I know that *Sincerity* loves not that it's Defenders should be indiscreet and rash: I know that the Passions of Men require Caution and Consideration—that they are

Maladies

Maladies of such a Nature—as to make it oftentimes necessary to cure the Patient in a Manner even *unknown* to *himself:* I am convinced that the grand Rule of *Zeal* in this important Matter—is Prudence and Charity. What we are *here* lamenting is —that so many Men should make a *Science* and even an *Honour* of Artifice and Dissimulation. Thus not knowing what Sincerity is *themselves*—they know not how to suppose it to exist in *others:* It is *their* deep Corruption of Thought, which renders the Sincerity and the Resolution of *good* Men *suspected* by them: It is a Disposition which appears to them romantic and ridiculous because that it is so great a Novelty; and as they find in it so much *Singularity*— they chuse to believe that it is Pride or Extravagance—and not *Virtue*.

Hence it happens, that we not only disguise the Truth, but openly betray it. This is the last Kind of Dissimulation exercised by

SERMON IX.

by the Scribes and Elders—a Diffimulation of downright Falfhood.

They do not content themfelves in quoting the Prophets in Terms obfcure and equivocal: Not feeing the three eaftern Sages to return to *Jerufalem*—they add (without Doubt to quiet *Herod*) that thefe Aftrologers afhamed not to have found the new *King, dared* not to appear in *Jerufalem* again—that they were Strangers but little verfed in the Knowledge of the Law and the Prophets—and that the Light from Heaven which they pretended to *obey,* was only a vulgar Illufion, and the fuperftitious Prejudice of a grofs and credulous Nation. And it was very artful in the Scribes and Elders to maintain this Language to *Herod*; becaufe they themfelves acted agreeably to it, in not going to *Bethlehem* to feek their new born King, and in perfuading *Herod* that there was more of

Credulity

Credulity than of *Truth* in the ſuperſtitious Reſearch of the wiſe Men.

See then what we, at Length, arrive at! *Obliged,* as it were, to humour the Paſſions of Mankind, and to pleaſe them at the Expence of *Truth*—we at laſt *openly renounce* the Truth: As ſoon as *it* incommodes us—expoſes us—places us behind a Cloud—renders us diſagreeable to the World—*then* we *openly diſavow* it; we profeſs to know nothing at all of it—we give it up to Oppreſſion and Injuſtice. Thus we form for *ourſelves* an *Heart* cowardly and ſervile, to which the *uſeful Lie* is henceforth a *Virtue*—an Heart *artificial* and *pliant,* which aſſumes *all* Forms, and which is never fixed to any *one* Point—an Heart ſo corrupted and ſelfiſh, as to make to ſerve it's *own Purpoſes*—Religion, Integrity, Juſtice, and every Thing holden ſacred amongſt Men. Happy *that* People, amongſt whom, Men of this Character and Complexion are seldom to be found.

I have only to observe by Way of Application—that it behoves us to take Care, that in attempting to defend the *Truth* and to prove ourselves Men of *Integrity*—we do not *defend* the *Illusions* of our own *peculiar* Temper. Pride, Ignorance, Infatuation, have *ever* been seen to give to *Error*—Champions as *intrepid* and as *resolute*—as *those* whom the Christian Faith so much and so justly glories in. The only Point of Integrity worthy of our Love, of our Zeal, and of our Fortitude—is that which Christianity *plainly* marks out to us: It is for *that alone* which we ought to suffer the Loss of *all* Things: In other Cases, we are Martyrs *only* to our own Obstinacy and Vanity. Let us then endeavour to honour this *eternal Truth* by a Sanctity of Manners: Let us *ever oppose* it—to Error and Vanity: Let us strive to annihilate in our

Hearts

Hearts thofe worldly Fears, which refpect *Vice* equally with the *Perfon* who *commits it:* Let us *ever* be *afhamed* to become a *feeble* Reed which is *turned* by *every Wind* that blows—but *never* be known to *blufh* in carrying *Integrity* written upon our *Foreheads*, as a *Title* the moft *exalted*, and as a *Mark* the moft *expreffive*, by which we can glorify *God*, and regard and benefit *Mankind*.

SERMON X.

UPON

The natural DESIRE of LONG LIFE.

PREACHED AT

ST. MARY LE BOW, on SUNDAY, OCTOBER 29, 1769.

SERMON X.

Job xlii. 16.

After this lived Job *an hundred and forty Years, and saw his Sons and his Sons' Sons, even four Generations.*

NATURAL is the Desire of long Life. *Job* indeed may at first Sight appear as an Instance to the contrary, who often wished for Death but it came not—who digged for it more than for hidden Treasures. Many others likewise have done the same I suppose; but upon Examination we shall generally find that such Wishes have been issued forth in the Spirit of *Passion,* not in the *cooler* Moments of Reflection. At *best* this Conduct is but *Cowardice,* and in *general* it is *sinful.* Cowardice it certainly was even in *Job,* severe as his Trials were; but as to the *Rest* of Mankind, their *Cause* of Complaint is, for the most Part, so *inadequate* to the Complaint *itself,* that when Men *thus* wish to die on Account of their *Troubles* and *Disappointments*—they doubtless sin greatly, and may justly expect as a Punishment for their Rashness—an Addition to their Misfortunes and Sorrow.

We seldom desire to die, when Life goes on agreeably; only when our Expectations are frustrated, and when Trouble is nigh at Hand. We never hear *even a Job* crying out, "my Soul is weary of my Life"— after the Lord was pleased to turn his Captivity, and to give him twice as much as he had before.

To

SERMON X.

To what then shall we impute this strong Desire of living to be old? To the general Pleasures of human Life? Or to the *peculiar* Pleasures which old Age brings along with it? To it's superiour Virtue—Dignity, and Experience? That it disqualifies us for the idle and vicious Entertainments of younger Life, and teaches us (in order to consult our own Mortality) to visit the Tombs of those of our Friends and Acquaintance, who have long since suffered Corruption? Do we *wish* to live *long* from a pleasing Attention to a rising Progeny? Or lastly, does not the natural *Desire* of *living*—proceed principally from the natural *Fear* of *dying?* This *Fear* I think equally *natural*, with this *Desire*—insomuch that I never wish to recommend or experience (as a mortal Being) a *philosophical Contempt* of Death. In *this* World I own that *Death has* its *Sting*, the *Grave* it's *Victory*. When indeed we have shot the

Gulph and finished *well*, the triumphant Exclamations—O Death where is thy Sting! O Grave where is thy Victory! will happily become us—but not *before*. I have been *here* speaking as *a Man*—yet, I trust, not *foolishly*.

But suppose we now make brief Inquiry into the Nature of old Age, and mark out Means by which it may become light and easy to be borne, and reverenced also by the generous Part of Mankind.

The just Creator of all Things—though he suffered Man to fall, and to be ever *capable* of falling during his Existence in this World; though he has ordained that Man shall be *born* in *Sorrow* and permits the Commission of so much Evil, that without great Care he may *live and die also* in Sorrow; has, nevertheless, amply provided Man with Instruments of Defence against all the Mischiefs which can possibly happen to him. In *every Part of* Life this is apparently

parently the Case, yea, in the *extremeſt* old Age the Reflection is infallibly true. But would it not be cenſuring the Deity to imagine otherwiſe? To imagine that he has given us Powers to *combat* againſt *other* Parts of Life, and yet leaves us *defenceleſs* in the laſt Act of it? It cannot be. Let not aged Perſons expect the Strength, nor thirſt after the Pleaſures of their younger Days: Age is to be regarded for, and to be made eaſy and comfortable by Means of it's ſuperior Virtue—Dignity—and Experience. Indolence and Inſenſibility are, I will allow, often to be found in aged Minds, but old Age *itſelf* muſt never be conſidered as *neceſſarily* inactive. Let us reflect (with *Cicero*) that Buſineſs of the higheſt Concern to Society—is not tranſacted by bodily Velocity, or Power of Constitution, but by Counſel and experimental Judgment: Upon which Account, Age is moſt fit to adviſe. In younger Perſons there is confeſſedly an

unlimitted

unlimitted Defire of Novelty—a Defire of altering (at all Events) what has been done before; which Propenfity too frequently begets Rafhnefs: Whereas *Age* being no longer fubject to the headftrong Paffions of *Youth*—is lefs liable to have it's Judgment or it's Reafon *perverted*. How many Inftances have we in Hiftory—within our own Knowledge indeed—of thofe who have paffed a quiet—an ufeful—an *engaging* old Age?

Happy and highly to be honoured furely are thofe venerable Characters who are free from Morofenefs and Peevifhnefs—but efpecially from *Avarice*. How common thefe Imperfections are to this Æra of Man's Life —need not be obferved: It may be neceffary indeed to *infift*—that where they are to be found *predominant*, it is owing to the Confequences of Habit and indulged Cuftom, not to the *unavoidable* Confequences of the State *itfelf*. As to a *fmall Degree* of
Morofenefs

Moroseness and Peevishness, we must, in some Measure, excuse it: Old Age, conscious of it's own Decay, is apt to be suspicious. Where there is any Fortune to leave behind, it imagines (and often with too much Reason) that it's Heirs shew an *improper* Anxiousness for the *Inheritance*; and where there is nothing to bequeath — being unavoidably the Cause of some Trouble, and of Course in the Way — it concludes that it is considered as an Incumbrance, and that the final Period of it's Existence is *impatiently* expected. Now to a Mind the least susceptible of Generosity or even common Tenderness — these Reflections must needs be exceedingly hurtful; nor should the World be too severe, if in this Case old Age betrays *sometimes* a Want of Chearfulness, and shews itself somewhat peevish and morose. As to *Avarice* in aged Persons, it is surely *altogether* without Excuse. What? When we have but a *little*

Way

Way to go, shall we upon this Account become the *more* careful to procure the Luxuries of a *long Journey?* Or because we have but *little Breath* within us, shall we exercise this in a greedy Anxiousness for the lavish Provision of a whole Life?

Here then let us consider our Subject in a religious Light, and discourse old Age upon the *moral* Act of dying. Methinks I see grey Hairs, with all the Infirmities of Age —startling at the Sound of Death. Yet why art thou so terrified, *good* old Man? Does he answer, " why callest thou me *good?* I am *not* good?" Nay, but thou desirest long Life, and God has been pleased to grant it thee: Thou didst not surely *wish* for this, *merely* to fill up a greater Measure of *Iniquity* against the Hour of thy *Departure?* " No; but I am unwilling to die " —unwilling to believe that the Warning " given to me by my trembling Nerves—
will

"will prove so very short." But why? Thy very *Entrance* upon *old Age* was a kind and pressing Invitation to thee, to provide for the Grave; and every Day since should have been considered by thee as a still further Indulgence of Nature; insomuch that come Death when it will—thou shouldest be ready to depart. * Young Men appear indeed to die, as when the Violence of a Flame is suppressed by the superiour Force of Water; but as to *old Age* like *thine*—*it* drops, as it were, *spontaneously* into the Grave: Nor should such an aged Person murmur, any more than the Husbandman after a plentiful Harvest—at the Approach or Arrival of Autumn. But continues the hoary Character before us— "the Truth is—I am afraid to die." Yet whence arises this Fear? from *Nature* or from Sin? "From *both*." Unhappy old Man!

* CICERO DE SENECTUTE.

Man! How abfurd have been thy Wifhes for long Life! What Advantage has it been to thee to fee thy Sons, and thy Sons Sons —even four Generations, perhaps, *go before thee*, fince thou thyfelf *now fhudderest* at the Sight of Death? What has been thy Employment? Where — thy Reafon? — that in *fo many* Years thou haft made *no Defence* againft this King of Terrors. In a Moment—unable to reply—he dies— looking as if he heard the Voice of his angry Judge proclaiming it through Heaven and Earth—" he dies, and let his aged Name for ever perifh."

Suppofe we fancy next another hoary Character in View, *chriftianly* expecting his Departure, *merely* from *extreme* old Age. Hear him then before he retires, to be no more feen. " I confefs myfelf to have been
" one of thofe who *wifh* for *long* Life:
" God has gracioufly given it to me, and
" I truft that I have made a *real* Bleffing
" of

" of it. But to effect this, I always knew
" that it was neceſſary to *bring* the *Means*
" of Happineſs *with* me *into* the State, not
" to expect that the *State itſelf* would in-
" fallibly furniſh me with them. On the
" Contrary, I muſt have ſeen in *others* the
" *Wretchedneſs* of old Age, when they have
" entered upon it without *one* Defence
" againſt it's Inconveniencies: I ever con-
" ſidered that a regular and upright *Youth*
" could alone qualify me for an happy *old*
" *Age*: I have far exceeded my threeſcore
" Years and ten, yet believe that if I had
" lived much longer than I have—I ſhould
" never have *repented me* of mine old Age:
" My *approaching* Diſſolution *troubleth* me
" as a *Man*—yet as a *Chriſtian* I am *more*
" than *comforted:* The *intervening* Paſſage
" has it's *natural* Horrors—*it* is a *bitter*
" Cup, and I *muſt* drink thereof; yet in
" undergoing this *ſpecial Exigency* of Na-
" ture I feel myſelf *more* than *Conqueror*.
                                  " O

"O happy Hour, when I hope to be uni-
"ted to that divine Company, who are
"enjoying perfect Bliss in the eternal Hea-
"vens! To those especially of my own
"Friends and Kindred—nay of mine own
"pious Offspring, whom even to the fourth
"Generation I have lived to see descend
"into their Graves." Having thus spoken
—let us suppose this venerable and christian Father to expire with all the Prospects of the happiest Immortality: Fancy him received into the Arms of his Saviour, and the Angels administering to him the transcendent Joys of Heaven.

Our Subject being of so tender and so interesting a Nature, I hope that a short Application more *immediately* to *ourselves* will prove both useful and agreeable.

What then are *our* Thoughts of long Life? Do we join the *Generality* of Mankind in *wishing* to *arrive* at it? If we do; that we may never repent of our Choice—

let

let us be influenced by the Example last represented—to go as early as we can, and do likewise. But the Arguments on both Sides *duly* considered; he is the *wiser* Man, perhaps, who *wishes to retire*—before Nature *leads him Home*. I can conceive it to be very possible for us to be *richly fraught* with *Virtue* and worldly Prosperity when we enter upon *old Age*, and yet to *suffer greatly* even from a Tenderness of Disposition. As *Thought* and *Reflection* are the *proper* Entertainments of *this* State, how may an Affection for our deceased Friends *break in* upon our *Chearfulness!* Again; altho' our *own* Lives may bear reflecting upon—yet it will almost *necessarily* happen, that *some* amongst the Number of those whom we loved *best*—. were unfortunate—either in their moral Conduct—in their Commerce and Engagements with the World—or in the *untimely* Manner of their Death. It is not unlikely that

that *Job himself*, blessed as he was with so *remarkable* an old Age, and however *qualified* for it his *great Perfection* of Character had made him; it is not unlikely, I say, that *even Job himself* was sometimes *wholly unmindful* of the Blessings of *this* Season of his Life, by taking into *tender* Consideration the *unhappy* Fate of his *former* Children.

And after all — tho' *long* Life should prove a natural Desire — let it be remembered — that *such Wish* is granted but to *few*. Our *infant* State is attended with a Variety of Circumstances which continually *threaten* Dissolution; and when we are grown to *Maturity*, we are oftentimes seized *so violently*, and cured with *so much Difficulty* — that it appears a Wonder almost — that *any* of us should live to be *old*. Let us then learn not to *desire* it — at least, not to *expect* it. And indeed — if we even set aside the Precariousness of the Tenure by
which

which we hold all temporal Advantages; yet our Hopes as Christians after Death, and the Difficulties which we unavoidably meet with Here being seriously weighed and considered —there seems to be no *real* Foundation for the *Desire* of living *long*. Nor do I think a Man justified in his *Desire* of *dying*, especially when he makes Troubles and Disappointments, or even *Pain itself*—the *Cause* of *such* Desire. When the Mind is heavily oppressed, or the Body racked with Pain—the Soul is apt, I will allow, to cry out for the Wings of a Dove, that it might flee away and be at Rest: Still, it is the Duty of the *Christian* to inform the *Man* —that he errs in *thus* wishing to forsake his Standard, till God thinks fit to send the Summons, and order his Dismission. And it may here be very proper to remark, that when a murmuring Spirit has once taken possession of us—we are disposed to see

all

all Objects in a *disagreeable* Light—to be out of Humour with human Nature *in general* from our own *particular* Feelings and Sufferings—and to insist as Madmen and Brutes rather than as Christians—that " the Day of Death is better than the Day " of one's Birth."

The true Spirit of Christianity respecting the Matter in Question is clearly this ——Neither to wish for *Life* nor for *Death*—to be *grateful* for Life whilst we *can* enjoy or preserve it; and to be ready with *equal Gratitude* to deliver it up—when Nature shall become *irreparable*, or when the God of Nature manifestly calleth for it. This Disposition happily implies a moral *Preparation* for *old Age*, if God should be pleased to bestow upon us *such* Length of Days: Or should he ordain *otherwise*—that we be cut off *sooner*, even in the *Prime* of Life; yet I will hope that from *this christian* Readiness to *depart*, we should be found

found *equally preparing* for an *happy Eternity*. And upon Reflection, we could not be injured surely—in being made *so early* —meet Partakers of the Kingdom of Heaven.

SERMON XI.

UPON

The Folly and Danger of despising
RELIGION.

PREACHED

Before their MAJESTIES, on SUNDAY,
MAY 31, 1772.

SERMON XI.

1 THESS. iv. 8.

He therefore that despiseth—despiseth not Man—but God.

THE Apostle, in his usual—*affectionate* Manner, is here exhorting the *Thessalonians* to proceed in the Ways of Godliness—that they live holily and justly, and in christian Love and Charity one with another; informing them, that he who despiseth in these essential Points, despiseth not *Man* — but *God* — God, the confessed Author and Patron of all

all true *Religion*, and solid, substantial *Virtue*.

But as it will ever be right, perhaps, to apply a Discourse of this Kind as soon as we can—I shall now take Leave of the *Thessalonians*, and address myself to the Christians of *later* Ages in the Language of the Text—He that despiseth—despiseth not *Man*—but *God*.

" One would be almost led to imagine,
" that some Men objected to Christianity,
" because it has confirmed every *Hope*,
" every *Expectation* of *Nature*," and made *secure* to us—the *warmest* Wishes of the *human* Heart. " *Nature*, with *unutterable*
" Groans, *pants* after *Immortality: Weep-*
" *ing* she sees her Children drop into their
" Graves;" because all *beyond* the Grave appears to *her*—*puzzling* and *uncertain*—a Land too *extensive* for *her* Knowledge—too *deep* for *her* Researches: When her Thoughts attempt to traverse *Eternity*
through

thro' all it's *variegated* Paths—"*now* she "*hopes*—*now again*—she *fears;*" and *thus* agitated by the *Viciſſitude* of theſe *oppoſite* Paſſions—ſhe finds no *firm*, no *ſolid* Ground whereon to *reſt* herſelf—languid, and wearied out by *vain* and *fruitleſs* Wanderings. How *different* the Proſpect which the Goſpel affords! *Here* we may view the *heavenly Canaan*—the *new Jeruſalem*—*that* Place of *many* happy Manſions, prepared for wiſe and obedient Souls, departed in the Lord. Nay, *ſo great* a Friend is Chriſtianity to *human* Nature—that it's Concern reaches even to our more *ignoble* Part—the *Body*; and not only during this Life, but to it's Recovery from all the *Diſhonours* of the Grave—to Glory, and Honour, and Immortality.

" Whoever therefore can *profeſs* to vilify
" theſe *happy* and *important* Truths, and
" to repreſent them in a *ridiculous* Light—
" he not only fixes certain Reproach and
" Infamy

"Infamy upon *himself*—he not only shews
"himself to be a *slight* and *careless* Obr
"server—but is in *Fact* (whatever his *In-*
"*tentions* may be; whether to gratify a
"*trifling* Humour—to display the *Archness*
"of his Genius—or *designedly* to corrupt
"the Morals of the *Age*.) Such an one is
"in *Fact* and of *Necessity*—an *Enemy* to
"*Society*, and the *general* Happiness of
"Mankind."

That Men are but too apt to indulge a *Propensity at least*—to a *Taste* of this Kind, nay and to conduct their Lives *accordingly* —you will, I dare say, with *me*, be ready to acknowledge. But that we may not appear morose and cynical—let us allow, that even *Levity itself*, in *some* Cases, may be *seasonable*, and *safely* exercised by the *wisest* and the *best* of Men: Still, altho' human Nature cannot at *all* Times attend to the Contemplation of *serious* Things—such as *God* and *Eternity*; let every Man be wise

and

and prudent enough *never* to make *Sport* of thefe *awful* Confiderations, fo indeed as *intirely* to lofe Sight of them in his *Practice*. Again, *Chearfulnefs* has *always* been efteemed a *focial* Virtue; and even *Raillery* is *fometimes* a pleafant Entertainment to *moſt* of us: Yet it behoves every man to chufe Subjects proper for Raillery; elfe he fhews a *wrong Judgment*—and makes his *Wit* and *Clevernefs*—Folly and Impertinence: This is as *offenfive* to Men of *Reafon*, as the Converfation of one who thinks it a Crime to *fmile*—is (for the moft Part) *dull* and *difagreeable:* However fond any Man may be of a *Joke*—he fhould take Care, even to be commended as a *Companion*—that fuch Joke be well *founded* and well *timed;* and as a *Chriſtian* and *good* Member of Society—*never* to give Way to Jefting upon *folemn* Matters, or upon *folemn* Occafions.

But

But what must we think of a Man, whose *Reason* is employed as a public *Advocate* for Vice and Irreligion? "Who *professedly* endeavours to set off the *Shame* and *Misery* of human Nature with false and *delusive Charms?*" Not only to be an *Infidel himself*, but to *labour* to make the *Rest* of Mankind become *Infidels* also.—— Not only to practice Vice *himself*, but to *approve* it *afterwards*, and to *recommend* it to the *World*.——O is it *possible*, that the Mind of Man, so capable of Exaltation, should ever *thus* have sunk itself!

As much, however, as Men of this Stamp may disturb the Quiet of the Community in which they live by their *open Profession* of Vice and Irreligion—yet the *Contempt* of the Matter, in which the *Pleasure* and the *Wit* are supposed *chiefly* to consist— the *Contempt*, I say, is levelled at *God*: He that *thus* despiseth—despiseth not *Man*, but God. And let us consider, that if the

Principles

SERMON XI.

Principles of Christianity should *happen* to be *true*; "the Man, who has so grossly "abused his Reason, as to employ it against "his *Maker*, and *all* that is amiable and "useful in human Life".—must surely expect to be finally treated with inconceivable Rigour and Severity. Let such an one suppose the insulted Redeemer of the World to direct a *secret* Arrow to his Heart whilst he is pouring forth Blasphemy; or let him only suppose those of his own flattering Community to attend him upon a dying Bed, "and to endeavour to banish his "*Fears* by the Relation of some *ludicrous* and "prophane Story;" yet how does he fancy that he should be *able* to *receive* it? Perhaps, instead of listening to these vile Deceivers, and in Spite of all his former Infidelity—he will *now* cry out, in a Kind of Delirium—what shall I *do* to be *saved?* And *despairing* of Salvation, extend *this*

Cry

Cry—to the Mountains to *fall* upon him, and to the Hills to *cover* him.

I will hope to be indulged with your still further Attention.

Far be it from me to recommend a *Wildness* in Religion—or to contend for Refinements *above* this World, or human Nature. The Christian Religion even *enjoineth* us to *use* this World, so that we do but always shew by our Belief and Conduct, that we have something *more noble*, something *more excellent*, which engages our *principal* Attention: The Christian Religion by no Means consists of one continued Course of Severities and Hardships, thus excluding Men from *all* the Comforts of Life, and dooming them, as it were, to an absurd and perpetual *Melancholy:* No; the Christian Religion is of a *chearful* Nature, and *embellishes* and *improves* the Blessings of *Prosperity*—whilst it affords a never-failing

Comfort

SERMON XI.

Comfort—adequate to the *severest* Dispensations.

To see then such a Religion as this—neglected and *despised*—must needs be *painful* to every one, who calleth himself a *Christian*—to every one indeed, who calleth himself a *Man*. We may be fully assured that the Christian Religion ought to be our happiest Consideration: " *It* is certainly our " *chief* Honour and Dignity — the *only* " Source of *inward* Satisfaction, and the Basis and Support of *social Good:*" Added to *all* this—it affords us the most transcendent Prospects in *another* Life. To submit therefore to the *Tenets* of *this* Religion as far as we are able—is not only meet and right, but the Height of Prudence also: On the other Hand, to profess an *open* Rebellion against *all* it's Precepts, is surely not only *inconceivably* criminal, but also *inconceivable* Folly: For we are here to be informed, that it is God who *promiseth all* the Blessings of Religion

gion, and not *Man*, who (at best) is only God's *Embassadour* in this Case: It is *God too*, who *alone* can fulfil *such Promises*. Since then to *God* should be given *Thanks* for these *noble* Privileges of our *Nature*; so by Parity of Reasoning, if we turn a *deaf Ear* to them, and *despise* them—let us not think that we hereby *degrade* a *Fellow-Creature* who may have been our *friendly Monitor*——for the *Contempt* is *(strictly speaking)* thrown upon God. On this Account it behoves us to be always very *cautious* of giving *hard Names* to *good Instructions*; and seeing the Christian Religion *in particular* so manifestly wisheth us *well*— what *serious* Man would *venture,* and what *wise* Man would even *wish* to *represent it*—as "the Effect of *Priestcraft,* combined "with the Cunning of *Statesmen* and *Poli-* "*ticians*—with a View to *enslave* and *impoverish* the Rest of Mankind.

When

SERMON XI.

When Men are inclined to give Way to a *ludicrous* Turn of *speaking* or *writing*—there are *Subjects enough* to be found in the *World*, without engaging in *Religion*. It is really so shocking to make *this* the Matter of *ridicule*, that I could conceive a Man to be guilty of *almost every* Vice under the Sun, and yet *shudder* at the *Thought only* of *ridiculing*—a *God*—*Eternity*—*Salvation*.

As *great Sinners* as Men may be—yet let them (at least) confess that they are doing *wrong:* As *little* as they may *believe* that they should be made *happy Hereafter* by a *contrary* Conduct; yet let them (at least) forbear from *despising* or treating with *unbecoming* Levity—the divine and benevolent Hand, which professes to offer *this Happiness* to them.

We, I trust, *have* taken Care to keep at the *utmost Distance* from a Crime so very hurtful to *cool Reasoning*—and to the Nature and Expectations of our *better* Part—

the

the *Soul*. I will hope that *our* Conduct in Life has *also* been (upon the Whole) *becoming those* who are *persuaded* that they shall live in a *future State*, and who *fully* believe in *future Rewards and Punishments*; and that even with Regard to those Vices and Imperfections to which we may be *severally* addicted—let me *hope likewise*, that we are always serious and *generous* enough to *own*—that we *wish* we were *without* them; and that the *yielding* to them—requires some Concession to *that God*, if not to *that World*, against whom they are committed.

And when *Religion* is the Subject of *our Conversation* or *Correspondence*—I am willing to think that we *faithfully* defend *all* Points " which describe *Virtue* in it's *pro-*
" *per* Beauty and Lustre, and strip *Vice* of
" those *artificial* Ornaments which hide it's
" *natural* Horror and Infamy: That we
" *strongly* recommend the Exercise of Justice,

"tice, Truth, and Benevolence—and *in-*
"*genuously* expose the *Mischiefs* of loose and
"ungoverned *Passions:* That we can, in a
"Word, at all Times trace the Footsteps
"of God's stupendous Wisdom and un-
"bounded Goodness—in the Works of his
"Creation—in the Conduct of his Provi-
"dence—and in the wonderful Scheme of
"our Redemption."

These are, doubtless, refined and exalted Speculations—the noblest Entertainment to our rational Faculties: And whilst we engage *thus* on the Side of *Religion,* we shall never suffer ourselves to be *bantered* out of our *Duty*; but shall always have Security at Hand against the most dangerous *Delusions,* which could *essentially* affect our *Happiness*—and may in our Lord's own Sense of the Expression, be *hereby* said to have chosen that *good* Part—which shall *never* be taken from us.

SERMON XII.

UPON

The PENITENT upon the CROSS.

PREACHED AT

St. LUKE's, OLD STREET, on SUNDAY, JULY 3, 1774.

SERMON XII.

LUKE xxiii. 42, 43.

And he said unto Jesus—Lord, remember me when thou comest into thy Kingdom: And Jesus said, Verily I say unto thee—to Day shalt thou be with me—in Paradise.

I HAVE chosen for our present Meditation—the striking Example of the Penitent upon the Cross. A pleasing—a truly comfortable Scene this—to every sincere, *practical Believer:* But what a Misfortune is it—that Men should build such a Confidence on the Acceptance of this Penitent—as appears manifestly inconsistent

sistent with the Word of God, and the immutable Conditions of Salvation! I must therefore desire your *particular* Attention, whilst I state this Matter to you in a clear and reasonable Light.

To grant at once the Whole that can be contended for with Regard to the Penitent himself—we will allow that his Salvation was *begun* and *completed* at the *Cross*. Still, how much more equitable was *his* Plea of Acceptance, than any which the *Christian of these Days* can make, who cries out for Salvation *only* at the very Gate of Eternity! How justly might *he* have lamented (as, probably, he *did* lament) the Unhappiness of a whole Life spent in the dark Mazes of Ignorance and Error—destitute of a Guide to direct him—and without the slightest Conception of a Christ or his Gospel! Nay, might he not, with some Degree of Reason, *modestly* have asked of God, why such Blessings had been *denied* him?

Not

Not indeed to *censure* the *Almighty*, but to make *his own Case* the *more affecting*: Not indeed to *command* Acceptance, but by *thus* addressing the Compassion of God—*earnestly* to *beg* it. And could divine Mercy do less than receive him? We will suppose that he was a *Stranger* even to the *Name* of *Jesus*, till he met *Him* at the Cross: Did he not then *believe*—as soon as he knew what was required of him *to* believe? Did he not *repent*—as soon as he knew what the Nature of *Christian* Repentance *was*?

But if we suppose otherwise, and that divine Mercy was exercised with *manifest Partiality* towards this repenting Malefactor: Yet even in this Case, no Encouragement can be given to the Rest of Mankind from such an Example. Infinite Holiness and a condemned Criminal were going to be crucified *together:* This was an Event which never happened *before,* nor ever is to happen *again:* The *Singularity* therefore of the Occasion puts *the Rest of Mankind* entirely out of the Question; and the *Greatness* of the Occasion *even more* than pleaded for the *Acceptance* of this *repenting Malefactor:* For what could be so striking an Intercession in his Favour — " as for him to " leave the World — with the God and Sa- " viour of it ?"

Do Men, however, still insist — that a like Acceptance of the Penitent before us is offered to *every* expiring penetential *Christian?* For a Moment we will suppose this, and even set aside the Possibility of *sudden* Death. Yet here let Mankind recall to their Memories the mournful Example of the *impenitent* Thief. This Man had all the Advantages which his Companion *had*; and yet wanted even the Inclination to accept them: And how many Instances of this perverse and relentless Kind must we have heard of — amongst those unhappy

Wretches

Wretches, who have suffered at the fatal Tree! I am afraid too, that in the Course of my own Ministry—I have seen some of my Fellow Creatures so *hardened* and so *impenitent* upon a *dying Bed*—as to be *resolved* not to sue for a *Pardon*—by only crying out—Lord, Lord.

Again, how apt are *all* Men (however aged, however infirm, however afflicted with Pain and Disease) to flatter themselves with the Thought of a *Recovery*, or that Nature will hold out *a little longer*. Now upon our present *supposed* Plan of Salvation, how likely will *bad* Men be to take such an Advantage of it, as to postpone the *short* and *easy* Work of their intended Conversion, till it be even *too late* to put it into Execution! The penitent Thief (ignominious as his Mode of dying was) became happy in this *great Particular*—that the *Certainty* of his *Death* made his *Repentance* also *sure*—allowed him no *idle*

Evasions

Evasions—no *deluding* Prospects of a *more convenient* Season.

But I have an Argument to introduce next, which I think must very powerfully alarm the more wicked and sinful Part of an Audience. I would wish you then to reflect — that this repenting Malefactor brought with him to his Cross or Death-Bed — Senses perfect — Reason calm and sober—and withal a Body free from Pain and Sickness: Whereas how often do *other* dying Persons labour under Pains and Diseases so acute and so severe—that what pronounces them *human*—is their *Shape only*. Now instead of knowing, instead of being able to become *reconciled* to their *Redeemer* at such a Time as this—their own nearest Family Friend, perhaps, may be standing by their Bed-Side as a Figure *strange* and *indifferent*—if not *ghastly* and *perplexing* to them.

Suppose

Suppose then that the wicked Man is allowed every Advantage conceivable either from *Nature* or the Example of the *penitent* Thief; still, his Situation, when he comes to die, may prove an unhappy, because a dangerous, one. If he should be *hardened* — (insensible of his Crimes, and careless of what may happen to him hereafter)—then he will be sure to die like the *impenitent* upon the Cross: And if he should have the Power and the *Inclination* to reflect—yet he will perceive it a difficult Task, in a dying State, so to employ and manage his Thoughts, as to render himself *fit* either for *this* World or the *next*.

But, surely, the Case of the penitent Thief, and *that* of any other dying Person, born and educated under the christian Dispensation, are so *vastly different*—that it is Impiety itself to suppose that their final Acceptance *can* (upon any Terms) ever prove the *same*. The Means of Happiness *so long* denied

denied to the *one*, have been *offered* to the *other* from the *Moment* that he was capable of distinguishing *Right* from *Wrong:* As soon as the Door of Mercy was open to receive the *one*—he piously and gratefully sought Admission: Whereas the Door of Mercy was *always* open to receive the *other* —till by his own impious Presumption he shut it against *himself*. Nothing, I fear, but *extraordinary Grace* can save such a Man as *this*; and whether he who has throughout Life called himself a Christian without having the *Faith* of a Christian— or who in *Profession* has been a Disciple of *Christ*, and in his *Conduct* the manifest Disciple of a *different Master*; whether, I say, this Man, becoming a true Believer and a sincere Penitent even at the *Close* of the eleventh Hour—can be thought an Object *deserving* of extraordinary Interposition—— let any one in his Senses determine. I will only venture to add—that if it should be

the

SERMON XII.

the Design of God *finally* to restore the *most flagrant* Sinners after *this Manner*; the Gospel Injunctions are but of *little Use*, and the Virtues and consistent Piety of good Christians but of *small Advantage:* But, beloved, be not deceived, for God will not *thus* be mocked.

Happiest of Reflections surely — that *Christ* came into the World and died for Sinners—and that he now sitteth at the right Hand of his Father as Mediator between God and fallen Man! Upon this kind Redeemer of ours let us *all* depend, as Salvation cometh from none other. The best Men upon Earth cannot *claim* Forgiveness or eternal Happiness upon the Score of their own Merit: But altho' they cannot *demand* this, as having offered to God *perfect* Innocence, or Things of *equal Value*; yet it is but reasonable to expect that a just Creator will accept their *good Works*, and reward them *accordingly*. Indeed the very
Term

Term *Mediation* implies *some Merit*, at least *some extenuating Circumstances* in the Conduct of the Person or Persons pleaded for; and likewise a *Doubt* of Acceptance. Unless therefore we can furnish *Christ* our divine Intercessor with *some Merit*, or some extenuating Circumstances, on which he may *found* an *Intercession*——presumptious, I think, is the Resolve to *ask* it of him; nor do I see that *Christ* would deviate from *his Character*—if he *refused* to *mediate* in such a Case as *this*; nor God from *his*—was he even to *reject* the *Mediation*.

Here then let me mention the strange Inconsistency of some even of the worst of Men—in sending for their Ministers just at the *Close* of Life; only to make us Witnesses of their *mock Faith* and *mock Conversion*, and to implore the Sanction of the Church for Hopes of a final Acceptance with God, as *happy* as *that* of the Penitent

upon

upon the Cross. There is, doubtless, no Care more deeply incumbent upon God's Ministers—than to deal *charitably* with Souls upon the Wing for Eternity: But we are to *remember*—that we must deal *faithfully also*; must *so* order our *Counsels* and *Expressions*—as to cause *no* sick Man to *depart*—either in a *vain Hope*, or in a *flattering* and *delusive Peace*. Would Men indeed live—at least in a *Kind* of *Preparation* for another and a *better* World—*we* should *then* be *pleased* to attend their Death Beds; and our *Visits*, instead of striking *them* with *Horror*, and *painfully affecting* our own *Tenderness*, would *comfort* their departing Souls: And surely you must think—that *satisfactory* is the Task—when we *can* from the *general* Rectitude of the sick Man's *past Life*, (and *consequently* from the *Word of God*) with Safety *pronounce* his Peace *solid*—and his Hope of Happiness *certain*.

I hope

I trust that you see the Force of this Manner of Reasoning. To preach — and not to preach to the *Understandings* as well as to the *Passions* of Mankind — must *ever* be preaching to *no* Purpose — or what is still *worse* — to a *bad* Purpose. I shall therefore close the whole, with this salutary and *friendly* Advice.

Lay not the *least* Stress upon the Acceptance of the Penitent upon the Cross: It cannot possibly afford any of *us* the *least* happy Protection. If you really mean to partake of christian Salvation — be mindful of it — whilst it may be called — to Day. Remember that the Night advanceth *apace*, when it may be *too late* either for *you* to *ask*, or for divine Mercy *itself* to *bestow* — Forgiveness. The Change — the irresistible Change of Death — will soon take the youngest and the strongest of us from our *favourite* Earth — will soon hurry us to the Judgment Seat of
Christ

SERMON XII.

Chrift : *There* — will the Sinner (on *Earth*, perhaps, *inflexible*) beftow the *voluntary* Bend : *There* — will Pride (on *Earth*, perhaps, *exulting*) level *itfelf* with the *very* Duft. Nor would I have you deem *thefe* the wild Suggeftions of *Frenzy* or *Enthufiafm* — but believe *them* to be — what they really are — the Words of *Truth* and *Sobernefs*. May they *fo* operate upon the Minds of *every one* of us — *fo* influence our Lives and Converfation — as to induce the dear Redeemer (upon his own obvious and *general* Plan of Salvation) to whifper in our dying Ear — " let not thy Soul — let not thy Soul be dif- " quieted within Thee — *to Day* fhalt thou " be with *me* — in *Paradife*."

FINIS.

www.ingramcontent.com/pod-product-compliance
Lightning Source LLC
Chambersburg PA
CBHW031819220426
43662CB00007B/716